Lost Restaurants

OF

DOWNTOWN CLEVELAND

Lost Restaurants

OF

DOWNTOWN CLEVELAND

· · · · · · · · · · · · · BETTE LOU HIGGINS

AMERICAN PALATE

Published by American Palate
A Division of The History Press
Charleston, SC
www.historypress.com

First published 2021

Manufactured in the United States

ISBN 9781467140881

Library of Congress Control Number: 2021941612

Dedicated to the memory of Michael—my husband, my chef—who seasoned my life with love and laughter.

Contents

Preface — 9

Introduction — 11

A Platter of Places and People — 15

THE RESTAURANTS

Allendorf's Chop House — 33

The Allerton Hotel — 36

Alpine Village — 40

Boukair's See Sweets Restaurant/Parthenon/Pierre's
Italian Restaurant — 43

Captain Frank's Seafood House — 48

Casino Restaurant/Weber's/Roundtable — 51

Caxton Café — 54

Clark's Restaurants — 57

Cloverleaf Restaurants/Blue Boar/Pickwick — 60

Finley's Phalansterie — 63

Fischer-Rohr — 68

The Golden Pheasant — 70

The Great Lakes Exposition — 73

The Hanna Building — 77

The Hollenden Hotel — 83

Hornblower's Barge & Grille — 91

Il Giardino d'Italia (Chef Hector Boiardi) — 95

Contents

The Mayfair Casino	98
Mills Restaurants	101
New York Spaghetti House	103
Old Allen Theatre Restaurant	108
Otto Moser's	110
Pewter Mug	118
Sheriff Street/4th Street: The Place to Meet and Eat	121
Shop and Stop	127
Short Vincent	143
Stouffer's Restaurants	158
Sweetwater Café	164
Terminal Tower Site	167
Winton-Carter Hotel	180
Bibliography	185
Index	203
About the Author	207

Preface

I t takes a lot of people to run a restaurant. The same is true with writing a book. I was definitely *not* alone during this project. I am grateful to all the people who helped me get these pieces of history printed. In alphabetical order, they are:

- Bill Barrow, Vern Morrison and the staff at the Cleveland Memory Project helped gather the pictures.
- Tracy Belcher, Tina Crawford, Kay Hoebake and Shirley Wolfe played the critically important role of cheerleaders.
- Michael DeAloia helped dig up so many obscure pieces of information.
- Alan F. Dutka provided access to his picture collection and provided assistance in sorting out many facts.
- Doris Higgins acted as my chief picture wrangler.
- Marty Perry took on the task of chief proofreader (aka Ms. Red Pencil).
- John Rodrigue, acquisitions editor at The History Press, endured it all!
- Patti Thomin provided development assistance.
- Everyone who shared their restaurant memories.
- The Unknown Group—those I have accidentally omitted from this list in my diligence to stay within my word count.

And, of course, all the staff at The History Press who helped with the myriad details of getting this story from my computer pages to your hands.

I could not have completed this project without the help of this supportive group. I toast them all!

AUTHOR'S NOTE

Restaurant history isn't just about the food that was served in a particular eatery—it's about the people and events that made that place unique and special. Just like today, sometimes what made a place special was the food, and sometimes it was the drink. Sometimes, not surprisingly, it was a person. There have always been "rock stars" among us. A few lucky eateries hit the trifecta of special food, drink *and* people.

Besides the obvious history of these eating establishments, it's good to remember that restaurants would be nowhere without the food. Did you know that these are just some of the edible items that are connected to Ohio?

- Cheez-It crackers came from the Green & Green Company in Dayton, Ohio.
- Stouffer Foods started in Cleveland.
- Chef Hector Boiardi created Chef Boy-Ar-Dee spaghetti in Cleveland.
- Ferdinand Schumacher of Akron was a founder of Quaker Oats.
- Harry N. Stevens of Niles invented the hot dog.
- John Leon Bennett of Newark invented the beer can.
- Clarence Crane of Cleveland invented Life Savers candy.
- Edwin Beeman created (what else?) Beeman's Chewing Gum in Cleveland.

Besides food, you need ways for packaging and preserving—Ermal Cleon Fraze of Dayton invented the pull-tab can opener for pop and beer cans, and Charles Strosacker of Valley City invented Saran Wrap. Ohio and Cleveland have always been cooking up good stuff one way or another.

Anyway, the stories in this book not only tell the history of Cleveland's restaurants straight and simple, but there are also the tidbits—the stories in the history—that just plain struck my fancy, and so I share them just for fun. I hope you enjoy them all as much as I did.

Introduction

restaurant (n.): *1821, from French restaurant "a restaurant," originally "food that restores," noun use of present participle of restaurer "to restore or refresh," from Old French restorer*
—Online Etymology Dictionary

When Cleveland emerged, it looked like most New England villages of the times—a town center or public square with the town laid out around it. Even at this early stage, the Cleveland House (at the current site of the Renaissance Cleveland Hotel on Public Square) was the center of the new city's social life. Of course, there were other hotels and markets to serve the travelers' needs for bed and board:

- The American House, where General Harrison addressed Clevelanders in 1840 during his Log Cabin and Hard Cider presidential campaign
- The Eagle Tavern
- Cleveland Center House
- Belden's Tavern
- Franklin House, a stagecoach stop

Lorenzo Carter, one of Cleveland's first settlers, built its first public house in 1797. He got a license to keep a tavern just four years later. It became the location of the first social affair of the city: a Fourth of July celebration in 1801. Thirty people came to the party and enjoyed whiskey sweetened with maple sugar, fiddle music and dancing. One historian called this log cabin tavern "pretentious," but that didn't seem to matter to the "trappers and other 'non-genteel' people" who would work for whiskey and board there.

This was just the start of a "tavern boom" on the frontier. In 1807, Amos Spafford opened a tavern that later became the Wallace House/the Mansion House, and George Wallace opened a tavern on Superior Street in 1812. In just over a decade, the city was ready to receive visitors.

By 1829, Cleveland had "one hundred and sixty-eight dwelling-houses, thirteen mercantile stores, fifteen warehouses, four drug stores, one book and stationery store, nine groceries, six taverns, and about one thousand inhabitants." The city grew along with its citizens' appetites, and by 1905 there were 2,475 cafés in town.

Although citizens and visitors alike enjoyed the hospitality of the city's eateries and lodging houses, not everyone thought they were a good idea. Mrs. Rockefeller (yes, *that* Rockefeller) thought that hotels were "a breeding ground for evil, outlandish capers; the refuge of nymphs and satyrs." She may have been right—in 1837, Cleveland's first city directory listed a Shakespeare Saloon that promised "Falstaffian delights to its customers." But it couldn't have been too bad—most taverns were closed by midnight.

Throughout the years, the city has been home to more restaurants, beaneries, cafés, diners, eateries, grills, cafeterias, lunch counters, luncheonettes, greasy spoons, hash houses, chophouses, steakhouses, pizzerias, coffeehouses, estaminets, tearooms, bars, inns, taverns, hotels and street vendors than you could shake a skewer at. Many were headed by distinctive owners (hosts, maître d's and professional restaurateurs) who raised eating from a plain business transaction to an act of social artistry. They gave the prosaic purchase of food an environment of comfort and camaraderie. There were hosts like Bob Bernstein at the Pewter Mug, Tony Falcone at the Hanna, Marie Schreiber at the Tavern Chop House, Pat Joyce's Iggy McIntyre, Gloria Lenihan of the Cadillac Lounge and the New York Spaghetti House's Jim Brigotti. And who could forget colorful owners like Otto Moser at the bar named after him and Herman Pirchner at Alpine Village? They were arguably two of Cleveland's most colorful characters. These men made their restaurants not just a place for food, but a destination. Although each generation looks back fondly with a feeling of loss and nostalgia at the restaurants of their time that have disappeared, each new opening brings in another personality, another mouthwatering menu and another place to remember in their "later" days. But for today, let's give in to nostalgia.

So sit back, grab a snack and a drink and enjoy this culinary cabaret of food, memories, places and trivial tidbits in your hands. Oh, but before you do, you know the saying, "Life's short, eat dessert first"? Well, here's a little dessert story to get you started. (Okay, it's not about a restaurant, but who doesn't like Girl Scout cookies, especially when top Cleveland chefs get involved?)

The Girl Scouts' motto is "Do a good turn daily." On Saturday, October 22, 2011, Cleveland-area Girl Scouts gave the city a "good turn" with their 16th Dessert First Gala "dessert-off" fundraiser at the Great Lakes Science Center to celebrate their 100th anniversary.

The competition invited area chefs to create new desserts using the Girl Scouts' Thin Mints, Samoas, Do-Si-Dos, Trefoils and the other tasty cookies. Chefs from twelve participating restaurants competed for the top prize that year. Some of these culinary stars included Dante Boccuzzi (Dante), Kara Swortchek (Moxie and Red the Steakhouse), Chase Phillips (Bricco), Tony Fortner (Zanzibar Soul Fusion), William "Tom" Hurt (XO Prime) and Brandt Evans with Scott Coffman (Pura Vida). Judges chose the winner based on the taste, creativity and presentation of the new confections.

Apparently, the sugar highs of the chefs, attendees and judges didn't affect anyone's dedication to such an unusual food fest. The event continued in subsequent years and was scheduled again for October 2020 but had to be postponed to 2021 because of the COVID-19 pandemic.

Bon appétit!

A Platter of Places and People

There were many restaurants in Cleveland that came and went over the years—just like in every other city in the world. This chapter takes a short look at some of the truly "lost" restaurants that caught my attention and then left with little or no trace for me to find them. Some seemed to have just plain come and gone.

BISMARK CAFÉ AND GROTTO (411 PROSPECT AVENUE)

While Adolphe Menjou was making a splash in the movie scene in Hollywood, his father, Albert, was making a splash in the restaurant scene in Cleveland. Both men were known for their dapper image. Stuart Husband wrote:

Menjou got his dapper sensibility and censorious eye from his father, a French-born hotelier and restaurateur who had a resplendent moustache of his own, and, wrote his son admiringly, "was a stickler when it came to clothes." Young Adolphe was expected to enter the hospitality business himself but was hopelessly seduced by the impromptu movie shows his father set up on the top floor of his Cleveland restaurant.

Connected for a time with Weber's Café, Albert reigned at the Bismark Café (sometimes seen as "Bismarck"), which was described in *Hotel Monthly* as "a quaint eating and drinking house." Possibly the reputation came from the fact that five physicians met there for a "round table" discussion every Thursday at 5:00 p.m., partaking of the "fine, heavy, satisfying food."

Menjou apparently got into quite a battle with the waiters union at the time. The war raged for two or three years, with both sides determined to win. Unfortunately for Menjou, the conflict crippled him. He worked in hotels and restaurants in Pittsburgh and Cleveland during his career and served as the president of the International Stewards' Association. When he died in 1917, the *Hotel World* described him as "a good French Restaurant caterer."

By 1936, the Bismark's days were past. According to W. Ward Marsh in the *Plain Dealer*, one of the few relics left of the café was obtained by Dr. W.J. Klein, who was one of the five physicians who met every Thursday. As the end of the restaurant was drawing near, Dr. Klein picked up a green carpet footstool (one of many scattered around the room) and walked out with it. It became a fixture in the doctor's office, always reminding him of a time when "people took time to dine, continental style, and spent time over their food and around the table in friendly discussion…and of the…heavy, satisfying food of the Bismark in the hey-day of its existence."

CADILLAC LOUNGE (2016 EAST 9TH/SCHOFFIELD BUILDING)

Charles and Gloria Lenihan operated the Cadillac Lounge in the Schoffield Building from about 1946 to around 1970. The Lounge had two claims to fame: a wall mural by William C. Grauer and that it was Cleveland's first gay-friendly bar.

In a *Plain Dealer* announcement about the Lounge's opening, it was described as a "pretentious new cocktail spot" (without any further clarification). Owner Lenihan was listed as also operating Pickwick Lounge on Clifton Avenue and Otto Moser's on East 4th Street, as well as about thirty-seven other restaurants and nightclubs in the area. He hired Ward & Conrad as architects to design the $75,000 café. Initial plans included music by some of Cleveland's most popular pianists like Eddie White and Charles Ruetschi. When live music wasn't available, there was Muzak. The original space had been a shoe repair shop, but the renovations made the room look bigger with sixteen mirrors strategically placed to reflect the burgundy-red leather settees, the marine patterned aluminum grillwork, the blonde wood paneling and the soft hues from the indirect lighting system. Actresses Lana Turner and Mae West were patrons of the Cadillac while performing at Playhouse Square.

Cadillac Lounge, Cleveland's first gay-friendly bar. *The Cleveland Press Collection, Michael Schwartz Library, Cleveland State University.*

Grauer's mural was done in an Art Deco style and was later used as part of an exhibit by the Western Reserve Historical Society in 1971. *Plain Dealer* writer Glenn C. Pullen described it as being "on the torrid side." The mural was placed so it would be seen when you entered the lounge and featured "undraped paintings of Lady Godiva and Europe."

Its reputation as a gay-friendly bar was that it was "strict"—no dancing or walking from table to table, and patrons wore suits and ties and enjoyed the music. Patron Robert Wood described it as "a place where you could be yourself, and not have to wear the mask, and you could talk and camp with some of the other gay fellows." The two-story lounge was a chic bar that was straight during the day and gay in the evening. Its reputation as "proper" (requiring a shirt, tie and jacket to get in) and "courteous" was attributed to owner/proprietor, Gloria Lenihan, who "demanded decorum and civility in the first-ever openly gay nightclub in Cleveland history."

By April 1970, the lounge's equipment and liquor license were being auctioned off. The space was later a Beef Corral.

CHOP SUEY!

Apparently, Clevelanders developed a love affair with Chinese food around 1919, when the *Catering Industry Employee* (vol. 28, 1919) reported, "Chinese restaurants are springing up like mushrooms, and from one small place twenty years ago to all of 25 at the present time." The market was big enough that the Brandt Company (which supplied meats, poultry, fish and other food items and listed itself as the "largest hotel, club, restaurant and marine supply house in America") took out an ad in the *Chinese Student's Monthly* (vol. 16), announcing, "If you can't get quality locally, write or wire us. Ask any Chinese restaurant in Cleveland or Northern Ohio concerning our products." Under its ad appeared ads for the Pagoda Chinese and American Restaurant (719 Prospect) and the Peacock Inn American-Chinese Restaurant (304 Superior Street East), which was described as "Cleveland's most beautiful Chinese-American Restaurant." Other eateries that seemed to have come and gone without much trace include:

- The Mandarin Café (622 Prospect Avenue)
- The Chinese Pavilion (718–722 Superior Street Northeast, next to the Hollenden Hotel)
- The Gold Dragon (21 Public Square), which advertised "Fine Cooking and Excellent Service"
- The Far East (1514 Euclid Avenue)

THE FAR EAST CHINESE AND AMERICAN RESTAURANT, CLEVELAND, OHIO.

Postcard of the Far East Restaurant. *Courtesy of Alan Dutka.*

COLUMBIA RESTAURANT (108 PROSPECT AVENUE)

In the 1970s, many restaurants had floor shows with dancers in their go-go boots. Cleveland was no exception. Dance leader Tony Manousos appeared at the Columbia Restaurant in September 1972, but who knows where it or they "went-went"?

ELEGANT HOG SALOON (1254 EUCLID AVENUE)

Former schoolteacher Paul Martoccia opened the first Elegant Hog Saloon on Buckeye Road in Cleveland. In January 1976, he opened another Elegant Hog at Playhouse Square. Soon more of these restaurants were popping up all around the area.

The saloon was famous for its Hogburger—half a pound of chopped sirloin served in five different versions and priced between $2.50 and $2.90 in 1978. Other offerings included shrimp and "trough" salads made up of spinach leaves, chopped shrimp, hard-cooked egg slices, mushrooms and baked ham with a sharp creamy dressing. However, *Plain Dealer* reporter Cynthia Reece wasn't impressed. She claimed that it was made of a small portion of these ingredients. Appetizers included snails bourguignon (at $2.95 for six), consisting of the snails in tarragon and garlic butter, and deviled crab ($2.95). For those not up to the Hogburger, entrées included beef bourguignon and Wiener schnitzel.

The restaurant was decorated with illuminated stained-glass panels hanging from a ceiling of herringbone panels. There were bi-level booths and tables and gilt-edged mirrors adorned the walls. Prominent jazz artists provided musical entertainment. In 1980, the saloon had a unique happy hour. On Tuesdays, it offered wine tasting classes for five dollars. A lecture from a wine expert included samples of six different wines and cheeses.

The Euclid Avenue Elegant Hog closed at the end of July 1988. Surprisingly, the space was *not* turned into a parking lot. A new hotel was built on the site, and the restaurant's bar went into Kennedy's Cabaret in the Playhouse Square Theatre Complex.

FAT FISH BLUE (21 PROSPECT AVENUE)

Originally located in the Bradley Building at 1212 West Sixth Street, Fat Fish Blue moved into the space that had previously been the parking garage for the May Company. The original restaurant opened in 1993 and closed in 1995. The move to Prospect Avenue took place circa 1997; the new site was slated to seat between 200 and 225 people. It featured a wall of windows and multiple levels.

Fat Fish had a New Orleans style that offered dining, dancing and blues, jazz and rock music. Some Fat Fish Favorites included legendary bluesman Robert Lockwood Jr. and the All Stars, who played every Wednesday night until his death on November 21, 2006. Charley Christopherson also played there for thirteen years.

The restaurant's theme was written on the wall—"Let the good times roll"—and apparently it was taken very seriously. Band members were known to join the customers, and the general atmosphere was "a whole lot of fun."

Fat Fish closed its doors in December 2011.

THE FORUM

On a June day in 1931, the Forum Cafeteria opened on the first floor of the Rose Building at East 9th and Prospect Avenue. The newest link in this restaurant chain boasted a $300,000 investment in a modern, sanitary environment—this in spite of a looming economic depression. On opening day, owner Clarence M. Hayman greeted the customers with an orchestra in the dining room and gave tours through the back rooms. In spite of these fancy first-day offerings, the Forum was a cafeteria built on bargain prices and selling large quantities of food served up in big portions. It offered convenience and tip-free dining with a fast-moving double line serving system in a room that could accommodate 350 people. The Forum was renovated in 1964, when takeout service was added. It would become a Cleveland mainstay until it closed in May 1983.

This new style of restaurant was a trend that had started in the 1920s, and it broke away from the norm of full-service dining. It was part of a reaction to many changes in American culture and society following World War I and the advent of Prohibition. Men had been the main customers of restaurants prior to this shift. With the ability to sell liquor taken off the table (or bar), restaurateurs began to make their establishments attractive to families, working women and shoppers. Family outings were becoming popular, bringing new groups of hungry customers to the dining establishments. The Forum chain had outlets in Kansas City, Chicago, Los Angeles, Houston and Minneapolis as well as Cleveland. It made everything from scratch. In St. Louis, it boasted that it had its own butcher shop on the premises and served 1,500 to 2,000 orders of fried chicken each day! Its chicken pot pie was especially popular. During the Great Depression, the cafeteria-style eatery provided steady growth in the restaurant industry. Eventually, the cafeterias succumbed to the even quicker and cheaper fast-food outlets.

LAST MOVING PICTURE COMPANY (1365 EUCLID AVENUE)

When the Stouffer's at Playhouse Square closed in 1972, the site later reopened as a part of the Madhatter's Night Club company as the Last Motion Picture Company, a restaurant featuring "large-screen movies and loud music."

As the Last Moving Picture Company, it was a far cry from its roots as part of the Stouffer's family. This independent nightclub was part nostalgia and part 1970s disco fun. People loved it and were lined up from the Allen Theatre to its door by 5:00 p.m. each Friday. Part of the fun included beer dispensed from a projector on the bar and an old sewing machine found in the State Theatre that was turned into a table. Customers became part of the "cast" as they headed to the restrooms labeled "Best Actors" and "Best Actresses." Music was made by the staff and played out of old radios. Of course, with a name like the Last Moving Picture Company, there were film clips that changed every ninety minutes featuring highlights of old movies.

There was a bar and nightclub on the first floor, with a restaurant downstairs. Both areas were decorated in movie themes, with old movie posters on the walls and placemats made of movie cards supplied from a private collection of seventy-five thousand items. Upstairs on an old balcony, there was space for private parties. The game room was featured at the National Restaurant Convention in 1973. It was said that the game room was one of three unique ideas in the country.

Although it was known primarily as a nightclub, the restaurant had a good lunch crowd, and sandwiches were available for customers to make for themselves to eat in or carry out. The Last Moving Picture Company had a good run until about 1978, when McDonald's took over the space.

THE PHILADELPHIA DAIRY AND CAFÉ (69 EUCLID AVENUE)

When the Philadelphia Dairy and Café opened around 1886/1887 at 69 Euclid Avenue, it attracted a lot of attention from people on the street. It had to be gratifying to proprietor Samuel Gottwals to see people stopping in fascination at the bright griddle holding buckwheat cakes, wheat cakes, corn batter cakes and other varieties that made their mouths water. It was a "dining resort" that became more popular every day. By May, it was being called "one of the best and most largely patronized restaurants in the city." The owners not only seemed to be geographically challenged, but it also looked like their taste was limited, too, according to one writer, who claimed that it only served breakfast food—"real oatmeal, cracked wheat with rich dairy cream, eggs…and raised buckwheat pancakes with butter and real maple syrup." Other reports, however, described a more varied menu. In September, the restaurant began preparations for a season of oysters served "in all the styles, both old-fashioned and modern."

Whatever it was serving, the café had three dining rooms to serve it in and two "large apartments" in the back just for the women. The large dining room was available for both men and women. The rooms were "handsomely furnished and are the most secluded and homelike of any dining rooms in this city." The café sported electric lights so it could be open from morning until midnight. There was a steady stream of visitors from nearby theaters. The dairy lived up to its name with a special offering of ice cream made on-site "of the purest and best ingredients." Other offerings included rich Jersey milk and cream and strawberries or strawberry shortcake and cream. All of this at "popular prices as well as… artistic cookery."

By September 1887, the Dairy and Café was enjoying enough prosperity that manager Gottwals leased the two adjoining stores to the east. When they opened in October, the new rooms had been remodeled and carpeted. The front was mostly windows. One window looked onto "the largest cake griddle probably ever made."

It seems that Samuel Gottwals was very busy in 1887. Besides his work at the Philadelphia Dairy and Café, he became the proprietor of the Doan in the Doan apartment building at 238–244 Erie Street/East 9th, which reopened with an elegant dinner on October 30. The restaurant was improved with carpeting, steam heaters, electric lights, wall and ceiling decorations, and the kitchen was brightened up and outfitted with modern conveniences. Seating capacity was listed as 150. There were two entrances and four large windows on Erie Street. Meals were served day and evening and included a choice selection of meats "as well as all edibles in and out of season." Regular dinners were cooked to order, served from noon to 2:00 p.m. for twenty-five cents and included soup, oysters, fish, rabbit pie, beef, chicken, lamb, mashed potatoes, lima beans, turnips, apple pie, lemon pie, cottage pudding, lemon sauce, vanilla ice cream and apples.

But Gottwals didn't quit there. In February 1888, he announced that he had secured a lease in a building on the northwest corner of Euclid and Bond Street (East 6th Street), where he intended to open a new "first class" Philadelphia Dairy and Café, with the move scheduled for April 1. Along with the restaurant, there would be a confectionery and bakery. The location was deemed perfect because both the ground floor and basement were well lit and attractive, and there was space to grow in the rear block on Bond Street. The ground floor would be the ladies' lunch counter, the soda water fountain and the confectionery, with more formal lunch dining on the second floor. Opening date was planned for April 25, 1888. On its two-year anniversary in June, everyone was invited to a celebration of free ice cream and soda water.

But wait, there's more! Apparently in an attempt to take over the job of feeding the city, Gottwals & Company planned to open another restaurant at 208 Ontario Street on May 4, 1889. The dairy (described in the *Plain Dealer*) was called "The greatest and cheapest restaurant in Cleveland." Like the operation at Euclid and 6th, this one would include a home bakery and was deemed likely to draw a large patronage.

Strangely, after all that activity, Gottwals and the Philadelphia Dairy and Café (and apparently its offspring) seem to have disappeared from the city in the early 1900s. By the 1930s, the location near Euclid and 6th was the site of Clark's Paul Revere restaurant.

RAFFERTY'S MONKEY CLUB (MONKEY HOUSE, ED RAFFERTY'S MUSEUM) (ONTARIO STREET)

This saloon has to be on the list of the all-time most unusual Cleveland restaurants, and in 1905, it was just one of 2,475 restaurants in the city! It's probably also one of Cleveland's biggest mysteries. Although it is clear that it was already in existence in 1905, there seems to be no record of when it opened or closed. But while it was there, it had to be one strange place.

Ed J. Rafferty owned Rafferty's Monkey Club (sometimes called the Monkey House) at Ontario Street just north of Huron. A sign in the window advertised "A hard boiled egg with every drink." (Eggs at the time were eight cents per dozen.) A beer and "poor whiskey" cost a dime, but for an additional five cents, you could get a glass of the best brandy. Cocktails were two for a quarter. You could also get "Bullet Whiskey" at a nickel a shot.

Rafferty began showing free movies on Saturday nights in his saloon around 1905 in what was apparently an early variation of "dinner and a show," although this was more like "drinks and a movie."

True to its name, the Monkey Club actually had three monkeys that wandered around the saloon, along with several raccoons. There were three-legged chickens that resided in cages by the bar, an intimidating ape named Kye and a bear with a bad temperament that had been rescued from Luna Park (where his irascibility was apparently a liability). Even the inebriated customers felt threatened by the ape and the bear, although it didn't stop them from sprinkling itching powder on the ape's back or giving him beer to put him to sleep at night.

Less threatening was a "Kangaroo Cat" that spent his time at Rafferty's other establishment, the Stag Hotel on West 6th Street. The cat, which Rafferty purchased from its owner in Kentucky, had "out-of-proportion" legs. The feline's front legs were not quite two inches long, and the hind ones were about eleven inches. This disparity forced him to hop along like a kangaroo in order to move about.

On the second floor was a music hall. At 3:00 a.m., it was at its busiest. Glenn Pullen wrote, "Gay young blades with beruffled ladies would drive up in hacks." A wide variety of entertainment was available in the hall, including "barbershop baritones" and stars like Billy Broad and Harry Ward, who worked in minstrel shows.

Things must have been pretty rough-and-tumble there, which should come as no surprise considering the animals and people crowded into the place. Famous prizefighters were hired as bartenders. These included Hughie McCann, Connie Kelly and the "Human Freight Car" Ed Dunkhort.

Just when all this excitement came to an end remains another Cleveland mystery.

THE TAVERN CHOP HOUSE (1027 CHESTER AVENUE)

The Tavern Chop House was a popular spot known for delicious food, generous drinks and a distinctive atmosphere with excellent service; its popular manager, Marie Schreiber, acquired the restaurant 1954. There were comfortable booths in a room with framed paintings and stuffed animals on the walls. Schreiber said that she purchased the artwork and kept them in a showcase near the entrance because her customers "enjoy looking at these exquisitely-made things as much as I do." This attention to detail was clearly part of her success, which she said was due to "catering to the most particular people and doing it to the best of her ability." When Schreiber took over the Tavern in 1954, she changed the masculine barroom into a place where women could come and feel comfortable. What started as a room with no floor covering by 1964 had become a beautifully appointed dining room in one of the best-known restaurants in this part of the country. Surrounded by dark paneling, there were oil paintings in gilt frames and colorful bouquets of flowers throughout. A touch of the masculine atmosphere remained in the old rafters, elk heads and stone grill. Downstairs were the Peacock Room and the Driftwood Room, private dining rooms.

The Tavern became a place for business meetings between Cleveland leaders, socialites and politicians, a place where they could dine on steaks in a masculine atmosphere.

Erieview Tower took over the site of the Tavern, and so Marie Schreiber moved herself and the restaurant to the Hollenden House in 1965 and re-created the original atmosphere as best she could. The old location is now a parking garage.

MISSING AND MISSED

The reality of lost restaurants is that many couldn't be included here—you just can't cover everything in any one book or story. Here are just a few of the restaurants that couldn't be included:

- The Bistro at the Bond Court Hotel
- Statler Hotel's restaurants (like Swingos and the Terrace Room)
- Stein's Café
- the food vendors and restaurants at the Old Arcade, the Colonial Arcade and the Euclid Arcade
- The Blue Point
- The Beef House
- The Haufbrau House
- Lola's Bistro

They are still an important part of Cleveland's gustatory history in spite of their status as lost. We toast them all. Here's to the places that filled our cups, our plates and our hearts.

AND THEY HELPED!: THE RESTAURANTS WEREN'T THE BUILDINGS

When we think of historic restaurants, we think of the buildings where we went to eat. But it wasn't really the place that was important—it was the people who operated the eateries that made the difference, like Chef Boiardi, Herman Pirchner, Otto Moser, Michal Symon and the rest of the staff who worked with these legendary restaurateurs to make the restaurants the experiences they were. Here's a few of those lesser-known Clevelanders who put the spice in the meal.

Joseph Angelo

Every family of chefs needs a senior member, and in the Angelo family it was Joe. Brothers Bill, Carmen, Daniel and James all worked in the restaurant business. Garlic was in their blood *and* in their salads. Joe told his siblings that for a "good Italian salad," nothing could compare with a touch of garlic. These cloves of wisdom were shared in a little cooking session at the Allendorf Restaurant, where Joe was head chef. Joe taught all his brothers to cook, and each became an expert in his own right. Bill was chief steward at the Chagrin Valley Country Club, Carmen became assistant chef at Herman Pirchner's Show Boat at the Great Lakes Exposition and James joined Joe at the Allendorf.

Like most good cooks, Joe got his first cooking lessons from his mother when he was just a teenager. In 1909, Joe was fourteen when he left Italy for New York and immediately put his mother's teachings to good use as an employee at a restaurant that catered Caruso's parties when the singer was in town. Joe proudly recalled that Caruso liked the Italian salad and spaghetti, which he always ordered with small chicken livers.

Heading west in 1913, Joe arrived in Cleveland and took a job at the Hotel Statler. He stayed there for six years and then moved on to the Rathskeller, eventually making his way to the Allendorf, where he stayed for fifteen years.

Besides Joe's salad expertise, he was a champion at preparing clams and could broil 1,500 steaks in fifteen minutes. Truly a chef of many talents.

Fred Diebolt

Fred Diebolt was born in Cleveland in 1840 to Ignatius and Gertrude. Ignatius ran a bakery and grocery in 1846, but two years later, his establishment was listed as a bakery and tavern. Fred went to work for his father, and in the 1870 census, he was listed as "saloon keeper."

Fred branched out in 1871. He and a partner began operating a bottling works in conjunction with a saloon at 76 and 78 St. Clair Street. Over the next several years, the business moved and expanded. In 1879, Fred had a saloon and billiard parlor at the southwest corner of Public Square and a wholesale business at 47 Prospect. Needing more space, in 1881, he moved his liquor house to 133–137 Champlain. The three-story building gave him ample space to store whiskey and other alcoholic beverages.

Diebolt supplied wholesale spirits to the many German saloons in Cleveland, including Joseph Kieferle's Black Whale on Champlain Street, Albert Eisele's saloon at Superior and Bond Streets, Paul Heine's on Water Street, Fred Sheurmann's on Huron Street, Boehmke's on East 9th Street, Brun Schwarzer's on Lorain Street, Silberg Brothers on Columbus Road, Weber's 242 Superior Street, Grebe's on East 4th Street and John Naumann's on Ontario Street.

BLACK WHALE INN. KIEFERLE'S RESTAURANT. 119 PROSPECT AVE. N. W.. CLEVELAND

The Black Whale was one of the many German saloons in Cleveland. *The Cleveland Press Collection, Michael Schwartz Library, Cleveland State University.*

However, Diebolt gained unusual fame when he took active objection to the "Owen Sunday Closing Law." Frank V. Owen was a lawyer from Mount Vernon, Ohio. In 1887, Owen won a seat in the state legislature. He was an opponent of alcohol sales, and he introduced a measure in the Ohio House requiring that all saloons be closed on Sunday. It became known by his name.

This development hit saloonkeepers like a bad hangover. Sunday was probably the busiest day of the week for them. In the German neighborhoods, Catholics and Lutherans would attend church services, and afterward the families would head to a tavern for socializing, beer and a meal. Not only did this law disrupt the traditions of these working men and women, but it also was a definite disadvantage to the saloonkeepers as well; they turned to Fred Diebolt, among the wealthiest and most influential of their group, for leadership.

Fred said that they should defy the Owen Law and stay open on Sunday. He told them that if they all refused to comply, the authorities would have to back down. Twenty-one saloonkeepers took his advice, and when the first Sunday closing came around in August 1888, they stayed open. Unfortunately, the newspapers reported the plan, thus alerting the police. Diebolt and the rest of the tavern owners were arrested. Jury trials were arranged for each of them in the hopes that acquittals would help nullify the law.

But things didn't quite work out that way. For one thing, not all of the saloonkeepers accepted this strategy, and members of the Ohio Liquor League, a bottling co-op of saloons, refused to meet or recognize Diebolt's group in any way. To make matters worse, many churches, newspapers and prominent citizens called vigorously for the law to be upheld. The police were happy to oblige.

Diebolt was the first to be tried. Clevelanders watched in fascination as he was found guilty in his first trial. However, the verdict was thrown out because of unexplained "irregularities," and a new trial was scheduled. No luck for Diebolt—he was still found guilty. As he was a wealthy citizen, this gave the press and public much to speculate about—"How tough a sentence would be handed down?"

George R. Solders was the police court judge, a well-respected jurist and a man active in the city's German American community. That, of course, only added to the speculation about Diebolt's punishment. Many Clevelanders doubted that Judge Solders would hand out the kind of punishment he often gave to "poorer and less influential men," according to a *New York Times* story on November 19, 1882.

Solders surprised everyone when he fined Diebolt $100 (a large sum at the time) and sentenced him to ten days in the Cleveland workhouse for violation of the Owen Law. Diebolt did not back down. He declared that he would carry the case to a court of appeals and announced that he planned to leave town for a while. Meanwhile, the rest of the disobedient German saloonkeepers were left to face their own fates.

The results of the other trials and Diebolt's appeal seem to be buried in the past. Cleveland saloons stayed closed on Sunday until the Owen Law was repealed. Fred resumed running his enterprises and actually had the short street to his saloon on Public Square renamed "Diebolt Place."

For those who question the popularity of Diebolt's establishment, the *Cleveland Town Topics* of July 7, 1888, reported, "Some funny things happen at civil service examinations. At a recent 'quiz' of this kind for a government position, one man, in reply to the examiner's request to name some of the leading business houses in town, said: 'The Blackstone Block, Post Office, City Hall and Fred Diebolt's.'"

MEMORIES

Linda Heiden e-mailed me on May 3, 2018, to say: "I also remember, when I was older, going with my father and mother to East 9th Street where we'd eat at the Forum Cafeteria. I think it was two levels, and we'd eat upstairs. I remember how neat it was to be able to see the food before you ordered it, so you knew exactly what you were getting."

J.H. Flora also sent a list of memories on June 12, 2018, about assorted restaurants in the city:

> *Captain Frank's on the 9th street pier was always a good place to visit....*
> *Black Angus was at 14th and Euclid. Around 1970 the building was turned into the Rusty Scupper. The Rusty Scupper was one of the first to have a brick and natural wood décor....The Rathskeller was a bar and deli in the Euclid Ninth Tower (Schofield Building/2000 East 9th Street). Up until the time it closed in the early 2000s it kept the same décor and ambiance it had when it opened in the early part of the 20th century.... The Hanna Building, also at 14th and Euclid, has had a succession of restaurants in it over the years. All of them in the same, attractive space.... Boukair's Seesweet Restaurant just east of the Hanna Building was a popular place at Playhouse Square....Fisherman's Cove...specialized in seafood, including fresh lobster, and I remember it as the first really nice restaurant I ever visited. In the late 1970s, when I worked for Diamond Shamrock Corp., we would go there for lunch for special occasions such as someone's birthday. One story from that time was, when a group was leaving the restaurant following lunch, Crazy Roy snatched a lobster from the tank by the door, took it back to work and put it on his boss's desk. I didn't witness this, but the person who told me about it had no reason to lie and I knew Roy slightly and believe he was capable of it.*

THE RESTAURANTS

Allendorf's Chop House

1011, 1111, 1118 Chester

This restaurant is one of the bigger mysteries in Cleveland restaurant history. The 1111 address regularly shows up as the location for "The Allendorf Hotel," "The Stag Hotel," "The Chop House Restaurant," "The Allendorf Chop House," "Allendorf's Steak and Chop House" and other variations.

The Allendorf restaurant started showing up in *Plain Dealer* ads around 1923. By 1936, it was being listed as an "old established steak and chop house." It earned a reputation as a "meeting place for Good Fellows and Good Food" where the chef's skill produced "steaming platters and high-heaped dishes" that made it a standby for Cleveland diners. Other famous choices included corned beef.

Like other restaurants in town, Allendorf's suffered during Prohibition. Its ad in the *Plain Dealer* on January 21, 1934, happily announced, "After 14 Years of Drought Allendorf's Is in Full Action Again." With the legalization of the sale of alcohol, Allendorf's was happy to announce that its service bar had reopened, and it pledged to serve "only the best quality, which will be on par with the quality of our food during the past eighteen years. / With pleasure we announce that Frank McKenna / Who is renowned among connoisseurs of fine cocktails and mixed drinks, will have charge of our service bar."

Hans Allendorf's Café at 1111 Chester was considered the prime spot for sportsmen from all over Ohio during the luncheon and evening festivities. Hunters met for dinner and spent the time recounting their adventures

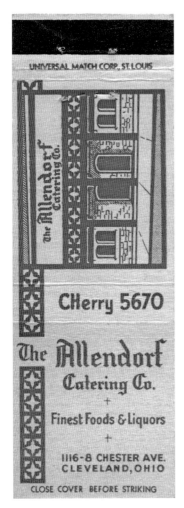

Matchbook cover from the Allendorf. *Author collection.*

as they hunted down moose, deer, bears, ducks and assorted fish and game. In 1937, the meetings moved to the new Allendorf Catering Company at 1118 Chester, where Hans took his post greeting everyone at the door. The wait staff, the customers and the "Tall Tales of the Trappers" all made the move to the new location across the street.

Apparently, Allendorf was on the move as early as 1924, when the Allendorf's Annex Counter Lunch opened at 1785 East 11th Street on March 10. A full-page ad was taken out in the *Plain Dealer* proclaiming that "Food tastes better at the Allendorf Lunch." Meant as the place to eat in a hurry, it claimed the same high quality as the original restaurant. Specialties included hot and cold sandwiches "fit for a King" and delicious homemade pastries, along with coffee and Tabor ice cream in an assortment of flavors to top off the meal. For the men, a variety of cigars was on offer as well.

As if the mystery of this restaurant's location weren't enough, it was also the site of probably one of the strangest attempted thefts anywhere. Apparently, Hans Allendorf decided to raise something bigger than a flag over his 1116–1118 Chester location: he put up a buffalo! A steer from a government ranch in Montana somehow managed to make its way to Ohio to be hung above the entrance of one of Cleveland's original sports bars. On the night of December 17, 1938, it was reported that at least two men attempted to take the buffalo home, apparently thinking that they could eat it (it was the Depression, after all). The buffalo burglars were foiled by the night watchman, who heard the crash when the bison hit the ground during the robbery. The men high-tailed it out of there, and the watchman retrieved a part of the blade that broke off during the emancipation attempt as the butchers tried to cut out a chunk of meat. Although the police were called, they claimed that they couldn't actually do anything since the men were gone and the buffalo was still there. After the wound was sewn back together, the buffalo was rehung above the door—this time with chain instead of rope.

In 1938, the Allendorf at 1111 Chester was purchased by Fischer-Rohr as the site of its new restaurant. After the sale at that site, John Henry "Hans" Allendorf operated Allendorf catering at the 1116 Chester site and at 1244 St. Clair until his death in 1948.

The Allerton Hotel

The Allerton Hotel (1796–1808 East 13th Street) was a 1926 Moorish Revival–style building designed by Murgatroyd & Odgen. It was later converted to apartments and renamed the Parkview Apartments. It was part of a chain of "club hotels" that provided a residential experience for young middle-income men and women and was meant to approximate a private club. These club hotels were described in company literature as "quiet, refined, club-like homes that provided socially respectable, economical housing for hardworking, refined, ambitious young men and women."

They were a variation on the more common "apartment hotel" buildings that were very popular in Chicago and other cities during the 1920s. Apartment hotels offered tenants the economy of small apartments and the services of large hotels. The hotel featured a swimming pool, a rooftop patio, a large coffeeshop and several recreational features. During the 1920s, the Allerton House Company was known as "the best-known provider of club hotel accommodations in the United States."

The hotel had a street-level cafeteria along the Chester side, and there was a main dining room on the second floor. The cafeteria was called the Coffee Shop and was open every day from 7:00 a.m. to 2:00 a.m.; it could accommodate 150 people. It also offered entertainment with a "small stage concept" that was called the Café Miniature and had a house band called the Three Musketeers. There was a lounge on the top floor that was particularly popular with the newspaper employees because many politicians and businessmen gathered there and provided them with stories. Afternoon tea was served in the rooftop solarium.

One satisfied customer was Elizabeth Doty, who stayed at the Allerton in 1942. She wrote that for $3.50 per day, she got a room with twin beds, a washstand and a toilet, and the showers were a few doors away. She also said that there were "all other conveniences (including a lobby of traveling men who ogle and 'eye' every gal that goes by)." It is unclear whether she thought this was an advantage or not.

At the height of the company's success, it owned and operated Allerton Hotels in Cleveland and Chicago and seven in New York. The Cleveland Allerton opened in 1926 and closed in 1971.

In 1926, the hotel was described as "a kind of show-business hotel," and guests included the Marx brothers and Mack Sennett's "Bathing Beauties," along with the Duluth Eskimos NFL team.

Show business remained a part of the hotel business. On July 10, 1950, actor-entrepreneur Ray Boyle created the Ring Theatre, which was rigged up over the swimming pool at the hotel. It was basically a summer theater, and its first season was well received. Its opening show was *Second Man*. Productions from that premier season included *Glass Menagerie* and *Candelight*. *John Loves Mary* and Moss Hart's *Light Up the Sky* included Boyle onstage. The *Plain Dealer* critic described the theater as "pretty good for the community...[and] adds very measurably to the sum of harmless pleasure in our community." However, in spite of what seemed to be a successful inaugural season, the theater disappeared after that summer.

In 1950, singer Holly Brooks was appearing in the cocktail lounge. At the time, the Internal Revenue Service had a cabaret tax that required businesses to pay when a singer "sang" *or* moved her lips when a recording of the singer was played (then they became a "pantomime entertainer"). As long as the singer stood there, played recordings of her voice, accompanied herself *and* kept her lips closed, no tax was required. According to an article in *Billboard Magazine* from May 20, 1950, it was speculated that the male personnel of the Cleveland IRS bureau would "probably keep their eyes glued to Holly's lips." In August that same year, famous burlesque ecdysiast and actress Ann Corio had a successful run at the Ring Theatre—in fact, they planned to extend her run. Although she had a slow start, her show was packed for the two weeks after the opening, and Ms. Corio did radio and TV publicity appearances, which obviously worked.

The Manger Hotel Chain purchased the Allerton in 1952. The Purple Tree Lounge was located on the first floor and became one of the "in places"

Manger Hotel postcard. *Author collection.*

Parkview Hotel, 2019.
Photo by author.

of the 1970s. The Tony Carmen Trio featuring Al Ginter and Pat Koshar played there Wednesdays through Fridays in 1970. The ultraviolet light in the room gave the colored tablecloths a bright white glow and made everything else black. In fact, it was so dark in the lounge that the joke was that if a guy picked up a girl there, he wouldn't know what she looked like 'til they got outside! Basically, the Purple Tree was strictly a cocktail lounge/pick-up place serving only bar snack food. In June 1970, the hotel was advertising that the Purple Tree Lounge would become the Gaslight Inn, but by August, the hotel was being liquidated.

Higher up the food chain was the Garden Restaurant on the top floor. It later became a semi-private "Artists and Writers Club," although anyone who paid the fee could join.

Both restaurants closed in 1971. The Allerton became the Parkview Apartments.

Alpine Village

Variously listed as 1612 and 1614 Euclid

Herman Pirchner's Alpine Village was best known for its parties and gatherings of celebrities and politicians; it also had live shows featuring artists like Pearl Bailey, Cab Calloway and Artie Shaw. But sometimes these stars couldn't hold a candle to owner Herman Pirchner. Born in Austria, the young Pirchner toured Europe as a circus clown, aerialist and strongman. He arrived during Prohibition in 1925 as a nineteen-year-old who couldn't understand why the United States had actually outlawed "a wonderful beverage like beer." Since that clearly had to be an error, he and his brothers, Otto and Karl, began brewing beer in the basements of Cleveland social clubs and selling it to the members. Soon he opened a speakeasy of his own at East 81st and Union.

The "jovial impresario in lederhosen" opened the Alpine Village in 1934 in Cleveland's Playhouse Square. Besides offering his customers good food with the beer, he had a dancefloor that could be raised and lowered. He hosted a parade of celebrities like Bob Hope and Dwight Eisenhower for dinner. Coast-to-coast radio broadcasts were done from the restaurants by NBC, making Pirchner's German accent famous across the country.

The Village's menu was mainly typical American favorites with featured German dishes, like glasses of sauerkraut juice, pig knuckles, bratwurst and German wines.

Herman's circus background took over when the Grotto Circus was in town. The circus manager complained about poor advance ticket sales, so Pirchner told him that he should "do something sensational, like have

Above: Postcard of the interior of the Alpine Village. *Courtesy of Alan Dutka.*

Left: Mary Tobak (*lower left*) and her daughters enjoy a night at the Alpine Village. *Top row, from left to right*: Betty, Helen and Irene. *Bottom row, from left to right*: Mary, Ann and Mary. *Courtesy of Ray Hudiak.*

Karl Wallenda [the world-famous wire walker] carry me on his back." The manager took him up on it and publicized the event to take place at Public Hall. Pirchner climbed up on Wallenda's shoulders for the death-defying performance. The two headed across the wire without rehearsal or safety net—fifty feet above the floor! Successfully making it across, Herman came down the rope ladder and fell flat on his face to the cheers of the crowd.

Pirchner was reputed to be able to balance fifty-five beer mugs while delivering them to the customers. He was said to slide into the table like a baseball player.

During 1942, there were many fundraising events for the war effort. In May, the Broadview Theatre on Pearl Road held an Army/Navy relief show with the Alpine Village chorus girls. The Village was one of the most popular places to escape thoughts of war during these years—this at a time when many patrons were boycotting anything connected with a German heritage.

Television created so much competition that many of the Playhouse Square Theatres stopped offering live entertainment. Downtown Cleveland became a ghost town. The Alpine Village began to lose money, but it hung on until 1956. Pirchner sold it in 1957, but he continued to run it until it finally closed for good in December 1961. The restaurateur died on February 15, 2009, at 101 years of age.

The property became the site of several other restaurants—the Americana Supper Club, the Eldorado and Rumors. Then the building was torn down. One less restaurant…one more parking lot.

Boukair's See Sweets Restaurant/ Parthenon/Pierre's Italian Restaurant

1520 Euclid Avenue/1518 Euclid Avenue/ 1524 Euclid Avenue

Boukair's See Sweets Restaurant (1956) was owned by Moe Boukair. As its name implied, it was *the* place for desserts and the best place to take a date after a show in Playhouse Square. Moe created the menu, produced the sensational sweets and designed the parlor fixtures, which featured pastel-colored lighting. The restaurant featured special sweet concoctions like huge ice cream sundaes, sodas, milkshakes and dessert cocktails. The names for these were as fanciful as the concoctions themselves: "Harem Shar'em," "Temple of Love," "Oriental Parfait" and "Snow Princess." Probably the most ornate dessert was the "Chic of Araby"—almost a foot high in an ornate bowl. It was truly ice cream art, with raspberry sorbet, coffee ice cream, marshmallow cream, toasted pistachios and dense whipped cream.

A decorative fountain sat at the entrance. Customers would toss coins into the fountain that Boukair collected and sent to Danny Thomas for the St. Jude Children's Research Hospital.

The iconic dessert spot closed in December 1973. In March 1974, Boukair took over the Adam's Apple in the Carter Manor Apartments (formerly Pick Carter Hotel). Boukair's was replaced the following year by the New York Steak House, which became the Parthenon in January 1974.

Although the steakhouse didn't last long, the Parthenon became an institution, providing sustenance to Playhouse Square visitors seven days a week until it closed circa 1987. Although Boukair's is listed at 1520 Euclid Avenue and the Parthenon at 1518 Euclid Avenue, at some point Pierre's

Postcard of Boukair's See Sweets Restaurant. *Courtesy of Alan Dutka.*

Italian Restaurant (1524 Euclid Avenue) apparently got absorbed into the Parthenon.

In any event, Parthenon owner Peter Shinohoritis had been in the United States less than a year when he and his partner, Andreas Salivaras, moved to Cleveland from Chicago, where they had worked at the Parthenon there. By 1978, Cleveland was ready to give the Euclid Avenue Parthenon the "Best Restaurant Award."

During its tenure on Euclid Avenue, it provided home-style cooking of standard Greek fare in a friendly and efficient atmosphere that was quiet and relaxed. Host Peter Shinohoritis greeted customers like friends, and Greek waiters were busy serving Greek wine and lighting plates of saganaki (a flaming Greek cheese appetizer), while bouzouki music played in the background. Travel posters of Greece hung on the walls. In the window, there were the spinning spits of gyros—seventy to eighty pounds of sliced-and-ground beef and lamb that was consumed daily. There were gyros and sandwiches of pita bread wrapped around a grilled shish kebab or onion that were $1.25 for lunch, with a gyro dinner at $2.35. Combination plates of eggplant moussaka, pastitsio (baked ground beef and macaroni in creamy sauce), stuffed grape leaves, roast lamb, potatoes and rice were $3.00. Greek salads ran $0.85. A family dinner not listed on the menu but available for

Postcard from the Parthenon. *Courtesy of Alan Dutka.*

Postcard of Pierre's Italian Restaurant. *Courtesy of Alan Dutka.*

$5.25 included egg/lemon soup, a saganaki appetizer, half portions of gyros, moussaka, pastitsio, stuffed grape leaves, spinach cheese pie, Greek salad, Greek-style potatoes, rice, dessert and coffee. The pastries were made on-site and included baklava and cream-filled galaktoboureko.

Besides the Greek food, the restaurant also offered live Greek music (Thursdays through Sundays) and belly dancers in the lounge Tuesdays through Fridays. In 1980, it was offering its customers a chance to learn Greek dances on Sundays.

After it closed, the building was razed to become a parking lot, and the restaurant moved to North Olmsted.

MEMORIES

Andrea Ranta e-mailed this "giant" memory on April 11, 2020:

In the late 1960s, Boukair's was still a popular place to go in the Playhouse Square area for people attending theater, going out to dinner or concerts, or those finishing off their evening from bar crawling in the Cleveland Flats. I had plans with some girlfriends to go out for the evening and we were all in our late teens, early 20s. Later, we decided to stop at Boukair's and check it out since none of us had ever been there before but had heard so much about it since it was a legendary institution! Having some ice cream to top off the evening sounded just right. It was late in the evening, but the place was very busy. We were taken to a table and given our menus.

The menus were rather large and the choices were overwhelming! What did I want to get? I not only could not decide, I was also distracted by spending time looking around at the different pictures on the walls of famous celebrities who also had visited and enjoyed ice cream at Boukair's over decades.

The waitress came over to take our order. I was undecided and still overwhelmed with the choices. Quickly, I noticed a photo on the menu of a banana split and I pointed to it and said "I'll have that." It took a little while to get our order, not that we minded as there was a lot to look at and talk about. The waitress finally brought our orders. When she put my banana split on the table, we all gasped! It was the biggest banana split I had ever seen! It was enough for 10 people, let alone just for me. Apparently, I had mistakenly ordered a banana split that was to be shared in a group!

I could not send it back! I asked my friends (who ordered normal size ice cream treats) to help me eat it. No way were they going to be able to do that as even their individual portions were significant in size! I felt people were looking at me to see if I could eat all of that ice cream. I couldn't believe that I had not noticed that the menu had a section listing larger servings for people to share! I never even looked at the price either! My girlfriends were shocked and hysterical! When they brought the massive treat to the table, I think my eyes almost popped out of their sockets. Needless to say, I put a "dent" in it, albeit a small one (hardly noticeable). It was warm weather, so melting was an issue to try to get the leftovers home. Therefore I spent an inordinate amount of money for a banana split that I'd never be able to finish even if I lived to be 100! As you can well imagine, I never lived that one down for many, many years!

FACEBOOK MEMORIES FROM APRIL 12, 2020

From Elizabeth Belle Buda: "Best chocolate marshmallow sundaes ever—and that Whipped Cream was the BEST!!!"

From Philip Kozimer: "Me vs their banana split! Won! Belly ache!"

From Andrea Campbell: "They had the best ice cream down town. And some of the biggest dishes."

Captain Frank's Seafood House

East 9th Street Pier

Come by car or come by boat. Diners could find a great restaurant regardless of their mode of transportation at Captain Frank's Seafood House. Sitting at the end of the East 9th Street Pier, it was the place where several generations of Clevelanders celebrated engagements, anniversaries, birthdays, graduations and all sorts of special occasions. There was a snack shop that served ice cream on the north side of the building. The building itself had its front door facing the city, but the dining room had spectacular views of the lake to the east and the west. With its nautical theme and spectacular views of the city and the lake, eating at Captain Frank's was more than just fine dining.

Frank Visconti came from Sicily and became the owner of the Fulton Fish Market. It didn't take long before he was thinking about more than just fish. In 1953, he bought an unused boat depot at the end of the East 9th Street Pier and turned it into Captain Frank's Seafood House the following year. The eatery was all about seafood, from its menu to its décor of nets, lobster tanks and trophy catches. For those who didn't savor the sea, there were chops and steaks.

Although Lake Erie is fresh water, upscale menu items leaned toward the ocean variety. In the 1960s, the choices included Broiled Live Maine Lobster with Butter for $3.50, Broiled, Stuffed Scampies in Garlic, Sherry Butter for $2.50 and French Fried Oysters with Tartar Sauce for $1.70. Lake Erie itself provided the main ingredient for Broiled Lake Erie Trout with Lemon Butter for $1.90. In spite of the expensive menu, Visconti had trouble obtaining a

Cap'n Frank Recommends:
KING CRAB A LA ROCKEFELLER

Split, buttered, and broiled, with dressing of bread crumbs, cheese and more crabmeat. Lightly splashed with Sherry. Served with melted butter, seasoned with garlic and parsley.

Postcard of Captain Frank's. *Courtesy of Alan Dutka.*

liquor license—Mayor Anthony J. Celebrezze thought that it would "create a 'honky-tonk' atmosphere on the Pier." After a mysterious fire at the restaurant in 1958, the license was granted, and it became a popular spot for late-night cocktails in the stylish bar in the 1960s. Perhaps it was the alcohol-free reopening celebration with all the politicians Visconti had invited that prompted the granting of the certificate.

The heyday at Captain Frank's ran from the mid-1960s to the late 1970s. There was a new indoor waterfall, and the restaurant became popular with young families, romantic couples and late-night revelers. Unfortunately, the eatery started to decline in the 1980s.

Visconti died in 1984, and the restaurant was sold to new owners who didn't really have the passion of the originator. Everything seemed to grow stale and sticky. The only high note of the decade was a cameo the restaurant had in the 1984 classic film *Stanger than Paradise* by director Jim Jarmusch.

By 1989, Captain Frank's was empty, and five years later, the building was torn down.

MEMORIES

Lynette Filips wrote on October 29, 2018, "There was also a restaurant even closer to the Lake on East 9th Street than the one in Erieview. It was called Captain Frank's, and was a 'casual dining' seafood place. I ate there in 1972 with the very small refund we got back from our income taxes. As quaint as it appeared on the outside, however, the eatery's food was a far cry from the sophisticated seafood restaurants in today's Cleveland."

Jan Springer wrote on July 9, 2018, "The story Carl likes to tell is about Capt. Frank's at the 9th Street pier. He took me there on our first date for steak and lobster (can you imagine steak and lobster on a FIRST date?). He ordered steak and lobster for me—I believe he had steak and crab legs."

Casino Restaurant/Weber's/Roundtable

242 Superior Street

Leonard Schlather was born on June 30, 1835, and came to America from his native Germany in 1852, moving to Cleveland in 1857. He got a job brewing beer at the Hughes Brewery, which he bought a year later, renaming it Schlather Brewery. He sold it in 1902 to start the Sandusky Brewing Company.

Schlather built the Casino Restaurant and Café in 1889 and opened it in 1894. At the time, it was hailed as "the finest restaurant in the United States." Designed by Lehman & Schmitt (James Rochford, contractor), the three-story Flemish-styled building cost $175,000. It had three floors with stained-glass windows and frescoed walls, but its most amazing feature was a hanging oak staircase. *Press* writer Winsor French wrote that to see "a hanging staircase drifting to the second floor with no support in one graceful curve, is alone worth going to the place!" It soon became a favorite spot for politicians, celebrities, newsmen and the public. The reason was simple: good food served in an atmosphere of rich, opulent, Victorian décor.

The dining room on the first floor was done in rich oak paneling carved in the Holland style and could seat 189 guests. The carved oak staircase went to the second floor, which had stained-glass windows, a banquet room (with seventeen tables), a smaller hall at the back with six tables and two family dining rooms for private parties. There was a lunch and oyster counter on one side of the room and an impressive bar on the other. A woodcarving of the family crest hung over the bar, which was an outlet for Schlather's beer.

Above and opposite: Stair details of Weber's Restaurant, now at the Atrium, Westlake, Ohio, 2018. *Photo by author.*

Other unusual features of the building included a separate entrance for women and elevators to the second and third floors. Originally, there were sleeping rooms for bachelors on the third floor. This area became the first meeting facility for the City Club of Cleveland. In 1913, the City Club rented the third floor, where it presented *The Anvil Revue*, an annual satirical production. Club members would poke fun at politics, people and institutions. The City Club moved out around 1916 to the Hollenden, and

the revue moved to the Duchess Theatre because of the growing demand for tickets.

The basement had a barbershop, a wine room, a supply room and a refrigerator. The room became a rathskeller and was later a disco.

Albert Menjou ran Weber's at the turn of the century. His son, future silent movie star Adolph, helped out. The restaurant was a fashionable place to go, and Menjou typified the formal elegance of the place with wing collar, frock coat and striped trousers. By the 1930s, things weren't quite so fashionable. Cleveland writer George Condon said, "Morose men used to wait on tables, using the thumb-in-the-soupbowl-technique." By 1940, Weber's was a second-rate restaurant, and its glory days were gone for good.

John A. Weber bought the Casino in 1904 and changed the name to Weber's. He and his son, Walter, ran it until 1927, when Ivan Kaveney bought it. Weber's closed after Kaveney died in 1959.

The eatery reopened as the Roundtable Restaurant in 1964 and was operated by Charles Lazzaro. Around 1974, it became a disco bar. Although it received landmark designation in 1977, Broadview Savings and Loan wanted a parking lot, so it was torn down in 1978. The famous staircase made its way to the Atrium in Westlake, where it still is.

Caxton Café

812 Huron Road

Joe and Allie Hanna opened the Caxton Café in November 1992. It had about forty-four seats and a tiny twelve-by-fifteen-foot kitchen. Joe was a restaurant designer who favored the Beaux-Arts style, so the room was informal but stylish.

After the Caxton Café had gone through two chefs in one year, Hanna hired Michael Symon, who had a good reputation in the industry. After Symon arrived, they created a whole new menu and began getting a record-setting number of guests for dinner.

At the Caxton, Chef Symon offered such delights as grilled salmon (wrapped in Swiss chard with wild mushrooms sautéed in white wine, chervil and shallots, served on top of asparagus) and veal chops on a gorgonzola risotto cake with arugula, sage pesto and frizzled leeks. Symon called his creations "New World Cuisine," which combined foods and flavors from all over and presented them with a stylized flair. However, friends called it "cool food." "It looks good, tastes good and is good for you." But beyond how good these dishes sounded, the visual presentation offered by Symon was one of the things that set him apart from other chefs—in fact, he was called a frustrated architect because of how carefully he built his dishes.

Symon took off on his own to open Lola's in Tremont, where he made his name as one of Cleveland's premier chefs. From there, his career exploded with additional restaurants, and he has branched off to host television shows and author several books.

Ali Barker replaced Symon in the kitchen, but the Caxton did not last long. It closed in November 1996.

Caxton Building. *Photo by Lee Groscost, Wikimedia Commons.*

MEMORIES

Interviewed on May 4, 2018, Nancy remembered:

When I was fifty, which has been a few years ago, Michael Symon had started the Caxton Café. For my fiftieth birthday, my hubby was out of town, and my son, who was quite young but worked at Great Lakes

Restaurant [Great Lakes Brewery], *got to know Michael Symon.* [He] *took me to the Caxton Café for my fiftieth. Michal came over and said, "Well, hi, Drew, how are you?" And Drew introduced us and Michael sat down, and I was fortunate enough to have my fiftieth birthday with two very handsome men....In fact, I think he brought me birthday cake or some type of birthday dessert. I can't remember what, but I know it was good.*

Clark's Restaurants

Clark's was a chain of restaurants in Erie, Pennsylvania, and in Cleveland, Akron and Youngstown in Ohio. It was founded by J.B.L. Clark in 1896 as a lunch counter on Bond Street/East 6th, and that was its only location for thirty-nine years. The original name of the chain was the New Dairy Lunch, although some sources list it as Clark's Dairy Lunch. Table service and a more "luxurious" setting were introduced in the late 1920s, particularly because women were eating out more. A.Y. Clark and R.D. Clark (sons of the founder) were in charge of the company in 1935 when they decided that it was time to expand. Soon they had opened more than twenty new locations. By 1966, an out-of-state corporation had bought Clark's and closed the franchise.

Clark's operated several restaurants on Euclid Avenue: 241 Euclid, 509 Euclid (in the Schofield Building at East 9th and Euclid), 1007 Euclid, 1520 Euclid and in the Hanna Building. They served southern colonial food and cocktails catering mostly to working people and families with children. The chain kept a treasure chest of toys at the front of the restaurant for children. In December 1938, it also offered a special menu and lollipops for them. Their parents could get a "Shopper's Lunch" of lima beans and eggs au Gratin, sliced orange and shredded lettuce salad, rolls and a beverage for thirty cents and "Fresh Apple Pie served in a bowl with Cream" for ten cents.

The 1007 Euclid location was opened in 1935 (east of the Union Commerce Building/Huntington Building). It was known as Clark's Colonial and was done in the Georgian style. The two-story façade was white brick and wood. Four pairs of double columns framed the building. It was the home of the

Postcard of Clark's Colonial Restaurant. *Author collection.*

beautiful Garden Room cocktail lounge and was noted for its charming door yard gardens.

Just east of the Williamson Building (BP Building) at 241 Euclid was Clark's Coffee Shop, with a lunch counter, tables, good food, modest prices and quick service. It was made for the person on a lunch break, not someone looking for a leisurely meal.

Theatergoers had a Clark's at 1520 Euclid Avenue. In 1955, the restaurant moved from there to the old Childs Restaurant in the Hanna space, where it stayed until 1965. It was known for its homemade pies and ice cream. The favorite was apple pie with cheese. In 1930, its trucks had a sign that boasted that it served 700,000 slices of pie in 1920.

Clark's Paul Revere House (509 Euclid Avenue) was exactly what you would think it was: a faithful reproduction of the home of the Revolutionary War Patriot. Features copied from the original Paul Revere house were incorporated into the colonial motif and included a replica of the Revere fireplace, antique colonial pistols and rifles hung on pinewood walls, hand-hewn oak timbers, colonial cupboards, plank oak flooring and leaded glass doors. The restaurant, housed in the former Burt's store (1936), was open from the 1930s until June 1947, when it was torn down and replaced by the new building for the Central National Bank (corner of East 6th and Euclid Avenue).

Postcard of Clark's Paul Revere Restaurant. *Courtesy of Alan Dutka.*

MEMORIES

Linda Heiden remembered on May 3, 2018: "When I was a little girl, I can remember dining at Clark's Restaurant. I think there was one on Detroit Avenue (on the north side of the street) in Lakewood, somewhere near Warren Road and I'm pretty sure that there was another one in downtown Cleveland on Euclid, maybe around 3rd. I remember that you could pick out a toy from a toy box."

Cloverleaf Restaurants/Blue Boar/ Pickwick

T hings change…and change…and change. It's not exactly clear what the whole story is for these restaurants, but it is clear that George Jacobs got involved with all of them eventually.

Restaurateur George Jacobs opened the Cloverleaf Restaurants in the Old Arcade in 1926 (which was still open as of 1956). In 1934, he opened the Pickwick Cafeteria "in conjunction with the Cloverleaf Restaurants," which moved to 238 Superior Street seven years later. A union campaign to organize waitresses in 1941 created quite a stir at this location for about ten months.

On September 1, 1955, Jacobs acquired the Blue Boar Cafeteria at 643 Euclid Avenue. In spite of an early statement saying that the name would remain, the Blue Boar's name was changed to Pickwick in March 1956. However, there's not much information about the Cloverleaf Restaurants or the original Pickwick Cafeteria. The Blue Boar and its subsequent reincarnation as Pickwick is the only one that left a slightly stronger footprint in the sand.

Originally, the Blue Boar was a chain of cafeteria-style restaurants based in Louisville, Kentucky. The first was opened in 1931 on Fourth Avenue near Broadway. During the 1930s, Guion (or Guyon) Clement Earle (1870–1940) served as advertising manager. He was the brother-in-law of Frank Kennicott Reilly (1863–1932), owner of the Reilly & Lee publishing firm of Chicago. Mr. Earle was well known to the customers of the Blue Boar through the witty jottings he created that appeared on the menus. A decade earlier, Mr. Earle had served as the superintendent of Loveman, Joseph

MAIN DINING ROOM BLUE BOAR CAFETERIA — 643 EUCLID AVE. — CLEVELAND, OHIO

Postcard of Blue Boar Cafeteria. *Author collection.*

& Loeb in Birmingham, Alabama. There he published a literary review titled *The Bookworm*, which apparently explained the creative menu-writing. Imaginative descriptions also went into its advertisements. In 1938, its *Plain Dealer* ad proclaimed:

> *When we first opened in Cleveland, we said: "The Blue Boar has a clearly defined policy—to serve the best and finest foods at the smallest possible price—just a penny or two profit per patron is not simply a phrase here but a Blue Boar creed." That is as true now as when we first wrote it. In a word you waste time shopping for chops—just come to the Blue Boar.*

Interestingly, the ad does not tell the cost of chops, but rather lists the cost of roast leg of veal as sixteen cents. An ad in the *Plain Dealer* on Wednesday, April 10, 1940, said, "If it keeps you smiling—keep it. Whether it is a friend, a book or a habit—keep it, and keep the pleasure it brings—like the habit of eating at the Blue Boar. That habit of eating at the Blue Boar will really keep you smiling—at the delightful food and at the economical prices." It was probably right, as the listing included prices of fifteen cents for roast leg of veal with dressing, salmon croquettes with egg sauce for ten cents, black-eyed peas for three cents and apricot chiffon pie for six cents.

The Blue Boar opened around 1935 at 643 Euclid Avenue and had an ornate main dining room with a seating capacity of six hundred and a back entrance onto Short Vincent. With Blue Boar catering to downtown shoppers, a *Plain Dealer* ad from February 17, 1943, declared, "Getting ready to go shopping? Remember the Blue Boar for lunch. It's convenient, it's prompt, and it's pleasant." Located opposite Taylor's Department Store, the restaurant offered shoppers menu items like Crusty Meat Pie with vegetables for fourteen cents, creamed salmon with noodles and eggs for fourteen cents and cherry sundae pie for eight cents—all this in the comfort of air conditioning. It seems unlikely that air conditioning was actually a selling point in February in Cleveland, but most of its ads, regardless of the date, mentioned this amenity anyway.

Besides its unique advertising, the Blue Boar had an interesting chef. Joseph M. Dulin was a chef at the restaurant in the 1930s. In 1942, he was drafted, went into the army and eventually became the personal chef to General Douglas MacArthur, his family and his headquarters staff. Obviously, the experience served him well because when he returned to Cleveland, he became head chef at the Blue Boar.

At one point, there were twenty-one Blue Boar locations in Louisville, Lexington, Memphis, Nashville, Little Rock and Cleveland. By the 1950s, the chain was facing increased competition from fast-food chains and changing lifestyles. Many of the cafeterias were located near department stores, and as these stores began to lose their luster in the 1950s, it added to the troubles of the chain. In 1955, George Jacobs took over the Blue Boar and operated it until about 1958.

At first, the name stayed the same and Joseph J. Prat remained as manager along with the 105 employees, but by March 1956, the name had been changed to the Pickwick Cafeteria. According to the *Plain Dealer* on March 10, 1956, along with the name change, plans were made to improve quality of the food in all categories. "Cleanliness and courteous service will prevail. Also extensive plans are now under way to greatly improve the physical appearance of 'Pickwick Cafeteria,' and at the same time simplify and improve our service." A postcard from the time declares that it served "Healthful food for the entire family." Besides the large cafeteria seating, the restaurant included a private dining room.

Pickwick Cafeteria closed sometime between May 1966 and June 1967, and a Newman-Stern store moved into its location on Monday, November 13, 1967.

Finley's Phalansterie

Huron Road Southeast and East 9ᵗʰ Street

Beefsteak dinners were a popular form of entertainment among wealthy businessmen in the 1880s. They even formed beefsteak clubs with traditions that went back to England and the early republic. At the beginning of the twentieth century, large restaurants and hotels had special banquet rooms for these feasts called beefsteak dungeons, dens, caves or garrets. Groups of men gathered for a night of fun free from conventional dining etiquette.

The festivities involved diners donning white butchers' aprons and eating the steaks with their hands while sitting on boxes and barrels in a dark, menacing-looking basement. Triangles of bread accompanied thick slices of steak, dipped in melted butter and grilled on a hickory fire. Usually the only other items on the menu were stalks of celery and mugs of beer. Eventually, pre-dinner sherry and appetizers made their way into the celebrations, and on rare occasions, women were invited.

New York City had quite a few of these beefsteak dungeons, but they were all over the country prior to World War I. Finley's Phalansterie was the Cleveland version. In 1907, a delegation of Congregationalists from Oshkosh, Wisconsin, arrived for a feast. Their review: "It was the most unique environment in which we ever took a meal, and although at first the novel surroundings startled us, the experience was thoroughly enjoyed." The dungeon's popularity diminished during World War I and Prohibition. However, one can't help but wonder if the memory of the

Oshkosh Congregationalists' trip to Finley's Phalansterie in 1907 explains why that city still had a beefsteak dungeon in 1939.

Cleveland's dungeon master, Richard G. Finley, was born in Detroit, Michigan, on July 29, 1876, and he became one of the city's most successful restaurateurs. Besides the Phalansterie, he owned and managed Finley's Central Trust Lunch, Finley's Depot Lunch, Finley's Ontario Lunch, Finley's Caxton Lunch and Finley's Bailey Lunch. These lunch places were very popular, particularly with the businesspeople of the city. Not surprising—after all, who can resist baked apple and milk? A 1908 *Plain Dealer* ad touted that all of the Finley eateries were offering baked apple at five cents, with milk. Choice King Apples were baked and turned, and "they certainly do look good and taste good."

So successful were these restaurants that, in 1910, Finley's annual income was listed as $250,000. Finley was a member of the Cleveland Chamber of Commerce, the Cleveland School of Arts, the Associate Charities and the Legal Aid Society. He was also a thirty-second-degree Mason. He was known as an idealist who gave time to pondering life's purpose and value. He encouraged the development of character and one's latent talents and powers. Author Samuel Orth described him by saying, "There is much of the philosopher and the poet as well as the practical man of business in his nature and his qualities are so harmoniously combined as to make his a most interesting personality."

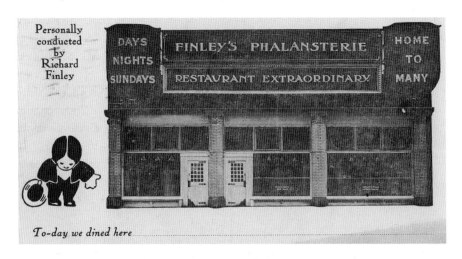

Postcard of Finley's Phalansterie. *Courtesy of Alan Dutka.*

Finley came to Cleveland with ten dollars in his pocket around 1896. He found a job as a waiter and, after several years, opened his own restaurant. By 1908, he had six big restaurants that were considered Cleveland's best.

Although Finley was a restaurateur, he definitely had a flair for advertising, which probably greatly contributed to his establishments' success. It was said that he advertised "every minute of the day. Not always with printers' ink, however." When his workmen were building his second restaurant, he put up a screen in front of the space to keep people from seeing what was going on inside. The sign said, "Here Finley will open a phalansterie." The amazing proclamation caused people to ask, "Who's Finley and what's a phalansterie?" For several weeks, Finley had them all guessing.

The theatrical advertising worked, and when Finley's Phalansterie finally opened, it was like no other Cleveland restaurant. Some claim that it was unlike anything anywhere—the furniture was dark oak, the walls had pictures done by the best artists in the city and the tables had fresh flowers. Downstairs, the dark basement was converted to a dungeon with an imitation cave at the back that was described as better than "anything ever seen on the stage."

After that auspicious beginning, Finley launched an advertising campaign that made his phalansterie, cave and dungeon known from one end of the United States to the other. He hired a salesman to visit downtown offices to tell the businessmen about the new restaurant and invite them to lunch there. He looked up conventions planning on coming to town and got lists of the delegates. He would then ask them to dine at Finley's. He studied the routes of the theatrical people headed to Cleveland and wrote to them as they approached to tell them to eat there. After they left, he would write again to ask them not to forget about him when they returned—they didn't! Soon Finley's was known to nearly every professional in the country, to people who came to conventions, to thousands of travelers and to all of Cleveland.

With this prosperity, Finley added more restaurants (he called them "systems") and publicized them by sending out booklets, mailing cards, blotters, circulars and letters. He printed new menu cards every day and usually had a quotation on them from some notable like Elbert Hubbard or Robert Louis Stevenson. Inside, there would be another comment or quote about the Finley system itself. The descriptions for the day's dishes followed, written in Finley's own unique style:

> *Boston Baked Beans—now there's a dish that has zest. Our chef is from Boston and—he does know how to bake them like they do in the Hub— individual dishes 10 cents.*

A corner in Finley's Phalansterie.

Postcard of interior of Finley's Phalansterie. *The Cleveland Press Collection, Michael Schwartz Library, Cleveland State University.*

And then there was:

*Bread—Staff of Life? French—real French Bread is—and we serve it—
all Branches—I used to wonder how they could subsist on a loaf of Bread
and a bottle of Wine—don't wonder now—Have the Bread—crispy—
baked thru and thru—it's better'n cake—Oh—yes we sell it—whole—
long loaves—30 to 36 inches—say 10c a loaf—best—we say best—you
ever ate—or money back.*

Finley obviously took the dictum to "sell the sizzle, not the steak" very seriously and literally.

The restaurateur printed so many things that eventually he opened his own print shop. That, of course, got him into the papers. His ads in the *Plain Dealer* and the *Press* were of various sizes and written in the same style, with a dash every three or four words. But Finley didn't just advertise in print. He had wagons in the streets that had signs saying things like "The Finley Restaurants—Ask any policeman for the nearest" or "Finley's—Yes Finley's"

The Finley establishments did not serve liquor, and the waiters and waitresses (called "clerks") were not allowed to accept tips. "Ordinary people" were able to dine at Finley restaurants for an average of twenty cents.

By the time Richard Finley had been in Cleveland for twelve years, he had six restaurants and was doing $500,000 worth of business or more per year. Leonard W. Smith in *Printer's Ink* described Finley's achievements as "something more than ordinary."

Richard Finley retired from the restaurant business around 1922. He became a real estate broker and dabbled as a stock broker. He died on January 2, 1937, of influenza.

Fischer-Rohr

1792 East 9th Street/1111 Chester Avenue

The beginnings of the Fischer-Rohr restaurant are a bit of a mystery. Apparently, it started as a food supplier in 1884 under the name of the Medicinal Wine Company, which later became the Boehmke Wine Company. Charles Rohr and E.A. Fischer bought the business in 1911. They continued to sell edible merchandise and beverages and had a large underground storehouse. This large "subterranean reservoir" was filled with mountains of food supplies that made up its stock of imports and domestic food items. It is unclear when the store turned into an actual restaurant. In fact, an ad in the *Plain Dealer* from 1918 still advertised its Christmas baskets for sale without mentioning the restaurant.

In any event, Fischer-Rohr opened at East 9th and Euclid in 1911 (the spot was later taken by Kornman's restaurant). Sometime between 1918 and 1920, it went from simply selling food items to offering table service. A 1933 *Plain Dealer* article described the company's pre-Prohibition activity by saying that it sold liquors, wines and beer for its customers at tables and at the bar, as well as by package and wholesale.

In 1938, Fischer-Rohr moved to 1111 Chester Avenue and changed its name to Rohr's Restaurant. The chestnut beams from the main dining room, the prism-glass windows and the hardwood panels were moved from the East 9th Street location.

The new space was designed by architect Leon M. Worley. It was described as a "traditional German Tavern" and featured windows made of bottle-end glass and doors of heavy oak with wrought-iron hinges.

Inside, there were paneled walls with heavy arched openings. The ceiling was beamed, and murals adorned the walls. Year-round air conditioning was available on both floors.

Rohr's was a favorite spot for lunch and dinner and served generous drinks. It had an eclectic décor with German elements and painted caricatures of famous Clevelanders. The private dining rooms were done in birch and walnut. Though known for its seafood specialties, including oyster stew and Lake Erie whitefish, the restaurant's lobster was called the "city's absolute best" by columnist Winsor French.

In November 1938, after fifty years of little music in the eatery, Rohr's broke tradition by starting Saturday night concert hours. Walberg Brown's string quartet inaugurated the new event with rich melodies and violin solos that worked well with the restaurant's old-world atmosphere.

Other than the mysteries of this restaurant's origins, Fischer-Rohr apparently had no strange activity inside its doors. However, it did take part in what can certainly be called an unusual, if not strange, event. Apparently, in 1936, the city experienced a rise in popularity of what the *Plain Dealer* was calling "neo-frontierism." One only had to look at the menus in the city's eateries to see the trend. Items like buffalo steak, venison and bear steak were being offered all over town. As if that weren't proof enough, the carcasses of deer hung outside several downtown restaurant doors.

Fischer-Rohr received what was thought to be the city's first delivery of buffalo for a restaurant "since the bowie knife went out of style as tableware." When the "delicacy" was unloaded, spectators lined the sidewalk and the street in front of the restaurant. The 1,500-pound beast would provide hungry Clevelanders with a quarter ton of steaks. Charlie Rohr said that the meat would be properly aged to be served shortly after the new year and that the buffalo head would be mounted and hung inside. It was also announced that anyone wanting to purchase a similar animal for their own culinary activities could get one from W.S. Caster in Missoula, Montana, for only $175.

A *Plain Dealer* reporter noted that contrary to the popular opinion that the buffalo was fast disappearing from the American West, there were now more of them than there had been in the last one hundred years. It is unclear how long this unusual food craze lasted, but certainly it proved a good source of eating and entertainment. Rohr's was razed in 1966.

The Golden Pheasant

944 Prospect Avenue

T
he Golden Pheasant Restaurant, next to the Winton Hotel, opened in 1919. This restaurant served American and Chinese food at moderate prices and included a large dancefloor with "a snappy dance orchestra." Throughout its run, it was managed by H. Kingsey Wong, who made it into a place known more for its musical stylings than its culinary servings. Chinese restaurants were among the first in the country to present live jazz, and Cleveland's Golden Pheasant was at the top of the list.

The restaurant underwent a major renovation and reopened on October 4, 1922, with a special "Guest Night" that featured the addition of a newer and larger hardwood dancefloor and an enlarged seating area. "Proper shades of light and appropriate fixtures" carried out the somewhat "Oriental" effect of the dining room. Other improvements included new plumbing and refrigeration. Festivities on opening night included an elaborate, two-dollar-per-plate table d'hôte dinner, with music and dancing by the Gene Reda Novelty Orchestra, souvenirs, confetti and prizes.

It was also the best-known Chinese restaurant in Cleveland to present jazz. The Austin Wylie Orchestra—whose members included Artie Shaw, Claude Thornhill and Tony Pastor—played there for many years in the 1920s. Radio broadcasts by Red Nichols and His Five Pennies were made from the eatery in the 1930s, and Bunny Berigan played there with the Hal Kemp band. A new arrangement of the spiritual "Jubilee" was written by Frank Trumbauer in 1927 in Cleveland and was first played by the Austin

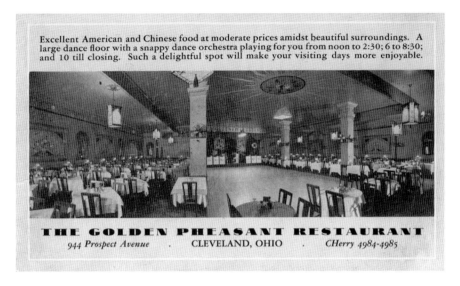

Excellent American and Chinese food at moderate prices amidst beautiful surroundings. A large dance floor with a snappy dance orchestra playing for you from noon to 2:30; 6 to 8:30; and 10 till closing. Such a delightful spot will make your visiting days more enjoyable.

THE GOLDEN PHEASANT RESTAURANT
944 Prospect Avenue . **CLEVELAND, OHIO** . *CHerry 4984-4985*

The Golden Pheasant was noted for its musical entertainment by top name bands. *Photo by Frank J. (Frank John) Aleksandrowicz, Wikimedia Commons.*

Wylie Orchestra during a WTAM radio broadcast at the Golden Pheasant. Artie Shaw joined the band in 1928.

Wylie's orchestra was described as "Cleveland's favorite dance orchestra, with a character and interpretation of music all their own." A number of big names played with the orchestra at various times, including Shaw, Vaughn Monroe, Kay Kyser and Merle Jacobs.

Abraham Isaac Arshawsky became Artie Shaw in 1928 and was a music arranger when he was offered the job with Austin Wylie's orchestra, Cleveland's top band at the time. Eventually, he became musical director. The band played eight hours a day at the Golden Pheasant. In 1929, Shaw entered an essay contest sponsored by the *Cleveland News*. The musician wrote a 150-word essay on "How the National Air Races Would Benefit Cleveland" and also wrote a song called "Song of the Skies." He won the contest. Shaw stayed in Cleveland for three years and then left to join Irving Aaronson's orchestra in California.

The Kay Kyser Orchestra and Isham Jones' Band also played the Pheasant.

The Golden Pheasant was clearly an important spot for the nation's jazz musicians. Not to say that food wasn't part of the entertainment. Though on the odd end of the spectrum of both eating and entertainment, the restaurant hosted the World Chop Suey Eating Championship. Finalists included Charley "Hallelujah" Holly, who came in second to "Suicide" Johnny Plummer (hopefully his unusual name had nothing to do with the quality of the food).

The Golden Pheasant continued to provide food and entertainment until sometime in the early '30s. It was taken over by George Shimola's Vanity Fair Club (which was originally located in the Flats) in May 1936, with Dolf Duerr taking over orchestra duties. The new club didn't last, and by January 1939, the *Plain Dealer* was reporting that the restaurant was being turned into a parking lot. Henry Wong, who had turned the Golden Pheasant into a landmark and an incubator for many noted bands, was then running two cafés in Washington, D.C.

The Great Lakes Exposition

The Great Lakes Exposition ran during the summers of 1936 and 1937 to celebrate the centennial year of the incorporation of the city of Cleveland. It covered more than 135 acres of land near the lakefront from West 3rd to East 20th Streets. Exhibits highlighted "the material, social and cultural progress which has been achieved in the Great Lakes Region in the past 100 years" and hoped to "indicate the paths of progress for the future." It featured all sorts of attractions, including rides, sideshows, botanical gardens, cafés and restaurants; in 1937, it added what would become one of its most famous features: an Aquacade of water ballet shows featuring celebrities Johnny Weissmuller and Eleanor Holm.

But what good is an exposition without food? The Great Lakes Exposition didn't disappoint—there was food for all. Along "Streets of the World," one could find two hundred cafés and bazaars reminiscent of the countries they represented. Since Prohibition had just ended, beer was big, and the vendors made every effort to accommodate their customers. There were many firsts at the fair. Jean Owen of Pepper Pike remembered that she had her first taste of orange sherbet there, while other Clevelanders had their first tastes of buttered ears of corn, corn fritters, fried chicken or Poole's grapefruit wine.

Herman Pirchner's Alpine Village Show Boat was smack in the middle of things at the expo. It was on a former ore carrier and was basically a triple-stage showboat. It had a supper club the size of a ballroom, and an El Dorado Club for members only. On the upper deck under a tent was the outdoor Polynesian show. The show boat was starting to look like a ghost ship when it reopened in 1937, so Pirchner decided that he needed to do something to make the restaurant and entertainment venue more interesting. Although the fair was supposed to be kid- and grandparent-friendly and nudity was officially banned, Herman decided that he needed to challenge that rule. He hired dancer Faith "Sizzling" Bacon to bring in the hungry sailors to the boat. Exhibition leaders threatened to stop the show, but Pirchner pointed out that the boat was in the lake and not on the exposition grounds and therefore exempt from the rules. The show went on—for a while. It closed when it turned out not to be as profitable as he thought it would be.

Billy Rose was the man behind the spectacle known as the Aquacade, which was housed in the Marine Theatre. Although its main focus was the Aquacade show, it could actually seat five thousand spectators and diners. Dining at the Aquacade was described in a brochure as sumptuous and reasonable "table d'hôte or à la carte, with cuisine directed by an internationally known chef." After dinner, there was dancing under the stars on a floating stage, with music provided by America's best-known orchestras. Demand for opening-night dinner reservations for May 29, 1937, was so great that a special telephone bureau was installed. In spite of its outdoor setting, bad weather didn't stop the show since diners and audience members could sit under a corrugated iron roof. Basically, it was a combination of water Olympics, Ziegfeld Follies and a Roman circus.

Rose's other restaurant was the Pioneer Palace, which had swinging doors that opened into a Wild West saloon. The walls were unpainted, and cattle brands and six shooters were hung up. Bartenders sported slicked-down cowlicks and manned a bar that extended all the way across one end of the hall. The stage floor was hidden behind the mirrors above the bar; they moved away to reveal the stage. The floor show was basically vaudeville. Lulu Bates sang period songs backed by a chorus line wearing Gay Nineties costumes. A sign above the pit pianist read, "Don't Shoot The Professor. He's Doing The Best He Can."

Other restaurants at the fair included an Exposition Cafeteria, which advertised, "Order a delicious, reasonably priced dinner at the big, clean, cool Exposition Cafeteria and let our hostess suggest what is inexpensive and interesting to see at the great Fair." For fifteen cents or eighteen cents you could get an entrée; for ten or fifteen cents there were sandwiches; coffee or coleslaw was five cents; and a slice of pie was eight cents. Clark's Restaurant ran ten hamburger and hot dog stands at the fair.

But *the* place to get your food fix was on the Streets of the World, where restaurants featured items with ethnic flair, including al fresco dining offered

Streets of the World entrance, 1937, Great Lakes Expo. *The Cleveland Press Collection, Michael Schwartz Library, Cleveland State University.*

Streets of the World was *the* place to eat at the Great Lakes Expo. *The Cleveland Press Collection, Michael Schwartz Library, Cleveland State University.*

at Frank Monaco's and several other bistros. The Grapefruit Winery was described as a "lethal joint" that served oversized pitchers of grapefruit wine for one dollar. There was also an African tea room, an Italian tea room, a Syrian delicatessen, a Spanish restaurant, a Slovak sandwich shop, a Syrian coffee shop, a Lithuanian café and a Swedish coffee shop.

An Armenian Village served kofte (a seasoned ball of lamb wrapped in an exterior of cracked wheat) and a dessert of baklava (a mixture of chopped walnuts and butter in a thin dough with fermented milk) and a syrupy Armenian coffee.

Other foods served in the Village included Russian borscht, Hungarian paprikash and stuffed cabbage, scaloppini Romana, ravioli à la Milanese and chicken cacciatore. As if all that weren't enough, by one count, there were more than a dozen doughnut outlets in the Village.

Most eating establishments also had some type of music or entertainment. The Hungarian Café served its goulash with a "gypsy" orchestra. Piano and song teams were featured at Alt Heidelberg. Violins, accordions and other string instruments accompanied the meals at Monaco's and Fortunatos. Like the rest of Cleveland then and now, it's hard to separate food from fun—and why try?

The Great Lakes Exposition stopped serving its food and fun on September 26, 1937, having served some 7 million people who brought in about $42 million to town.

The Hanna Building

East 14th and Euclid

The Hanna Building has provided food and entertainment for Clevelanders since it first opened in 1921 and continues that tradition today.

The restaurants in the building were located in a space on the first floor called "the grandest dining room between New York and Chicago." Designed in the Pompeian style, the center had a ceiling that was almost two stories high. The elegant space was lit with chandeliers, skylights and clerestory windows. There were fluted columns leading to other lounge and dining areas around the perimeter. The room was painted in earth tones complementing a terrazzo floor. Tabletops were polished, gleaming and left bare. More than three hundred people could be seated in the main dining room. The palatial setting and elegance created a memorable experience.

The first dining room opened in 1922 and was called the Hanna Building Restaurant. It became the Monaco in 1931 and was run by Frank Monaco. Frank's trademark was that he made his guests feel personally welcomed. Décor in the new space included deep colors and carpets of bold, abstract patterns. The clerestory windows were covered in ornate brass grillwork. The Monaco offered entertainment, and a large dancefloor and bandstand were added. In 1937, an after-theater supper package was offered for seventy-five cents that included the dinner, a floor show with the dance team of Ted and Mary Taft and other music and dancing. Frank left the Hanna in 1945 to open another Monaco's at 1118 Chester Avenue in 1947. The restaurant became the Continental Room with Frank's departure.

AFTER THE SHOW

Dine and Dance
at the

**Hanna Building
Restaurant**

Continuous Service 10:00 P. M. to 1:00 A.M

No Cover Charge (Except Saturday)
MUSIC and DANCING

SPECIAL TABLE d' HOTE DINNER
Complete in its Every Detail
Served 5:30 to 9:00 P. M.

Music
Dancing   **$1.50 PER PLATE**   No Cover Charge

Ad for the Hanna Building Restaurant. *Courtesy of Alan Dutka.*

In 1949, the Continental became Childs Restaurant, a popular New York chain known for having a chef flipping pancakes in the front window. Of course, the look of the restaurant changed along with the name. The twenty-seven-foot ceiling was lowered, and the plaster details of the room were painted over. The bold carpet designs were changed to simple geometric patterns. The space was divided into two dining rooms and two luncheonettes. There was a window on Euclid Avenue where passersby could watch the famous pancake flipping.

Childs stayed at the Hanna until 1954/55, when Clark's moved in. The eating space soon turned into a kind of functional American style. There were bare tabletops and plastic-covered seating as the room became a basic dining room. Clark's stayed until 1965, when it became the Pewter Mug/ Hanna Pub.

John Cardullias dropped the ceiling thirteen feet and eliminated the two Euclid Avenue entrances to the restaurant when he opened the Pewter Mug. In the center of the room was a four-sided fireplace. The wood columns in the room were redone in brick to reinforce the English Tudor style of the new establishment. High-quality food, fast service and "solid drinks" of 2.5-ounce martinis and Manhattans were featured.

The menu included a selection of steaks and lobster tails. If you didn't like the options on the menu, you could get a dinner not on the menu, like the eye of the rib, *if* you got a table by the wall all to yourself. Eye of rib is

Interior of Clark's at the Hanna. *Courtesy of Alan Dutka.*

what's left after the chef has removed the "less edible" part of a standing rib roast. It was served with a salad, a potato that was sliced and then put back together and fried and a whole loaf of pumpernickel bread. It could be served au jus (and one reviewer stated forthrightly that you had better say "yes" when asked if you'd like it that way). Why, you might wonder, would you have to be alone to order this delicious dish? To allow you to dunk the pumpernickel bread into the jus without embarrassment.

The Pub also had a private dining room: the Winston Churchill. The walls were lined with pictures of the British politician. For eleven years, it hosted the weekly luncheon of Ye Olde Cheshire Cheese Club, described by writer Peter Bellamy as "a group of wits and book lovers." The club was named after a London restaurant/bar founded in 1667 that was a favorite spot for writers like Samuel Johnson, Charles Dickens and James Boswell and the painter Sir Joshua Reynolds.

After the Hanna Pub, the space became Cuisines in 1985, owned by designer Roberta Rocco; her husband, Sammy Catania; and chef Pamela Grosscup. It returned the space to the original Pompeian style of the Hanna's first restaurant. Cincinnati preservationist architects Ken Jones and Thomas E. Speer tore out dry wall, carpet, acoustical tile and wood veneer from the old restaurant and uncovered plaster detail, moldings, structural columns, the terrazzo flooring, the clerestory windows and the skylights. Just inside the entrance was a music pavilion of free-standing columns decorated in geometric patterns. The main room was broken up with detached white walls to separate the bar from the dining room. The color scheme was done in white, sea foam green, creamy mauve and light blue, with patches of bright red. Furniture featured lavender and red, with tables covered in white linen. There were "Oriental" carpets (on loan from Victor Davidian and the May Company) and contemporary paintings from the Grosscup Collection. Softness was added to the room with pale patterned drapings between room columns and swatches hanging from steel grids. The atmosphere was calm with a sense of elegance. Rocco and Catania also ran Impromptu Cuisine, located in the Old Arcade from about 1985 to 1988, when it was sold to Man Baek.

The restaurant merry-go-round at the Hanna moved pretty quickly once Cuisines closed circa 1989. Getty's at the Hanna replaced Cuisines. Attached to the restaurant was Rhythms, a small supper club that opened on August 23, 1991. Opening entertainment was provided by jazz pianist Jeremy Wall, founder of Spyro Gyra. Opening night admission was seven dollars. The club seated 150, served food and had a stage for the musicians.

By the mid-1990s, Larry Mako and Cleveland Browns guard Gene Hickerson had bought the eatery and renamed it Hickerson's. Apparently, Getty's was a good model, and *Plain Dealer* reporter Wilma Salisbury was glad they didn't change much. The dining room was spacious and recalled the "elegance of downtown Cleveland in the 1920s." Along with the visual elegance, the ambiance was enhanced by pianist Pete Selvagio, who played cocktail music at lunch time and was joined by vocalist Leslie Lewis to provide dinner music four nights a week. Salisbury went on to describe the atmosphere as "relaxing and the service first-class."

Besides maintaining the Getty's atmosphere, Getty's head chef, Willie Banks, stayed on to provide the food at Hickerson's. Many items remained on the menu, including salad Brittany (mixed greens with grilled chicken, bacon and almonds in warm cognac dressing) and spinach fettuccini with peppery smoked salmon, red peppers and artichoke hearts tossed in a creamy pesto sauce. Also available was a selection of beef, poultry, seafood, veal, pork, lamb and pasta dishes. The lunch menu included deli sandwiches and burgers. A pre-theater menu of grilled entrées was available, along with a regular menu of more elaborate choices like Chateaubriand (twenty-five dollars per person), which was meant to be savored slowly, and surf and turf (for forty dollars), with filet mignon in burgundy wine sauce and fresh-tasting cold-water lobster tail served with drawn butter.

In spite of her initial praise, Ms. Salisbury said that there was inconsistency in the food served at the restaurant from the appetizers to the entrées. She went on to say that the dinner choices needed to come up to the high standards of the desserts of fresh cheesecakes and torts provided by a local, though unnamed, bakery.

By February 2008, the place had changed again. Now called Bricco, the new restaurant was decorated in a trendy tangerine color. It served pan-seared salmon that was caramelized golden on top for eighteen dollars. A full-flavored eight-ounce filet with tomato butter and garlic mashed potatoes was available for twenty-six. Salads were offered in full and half portions and included a salad of spinach, arugula, shaved fennel and grapefruit. Appetizers large enough to substitute for a meal included a crock of goat cheese with warmed spicy marinara, served with fried pita wedges; a mini-serving of seared duck breast on greens; and calamari and chorizo with olives. Desserts included a mango cheesecake with crème brûlée. One customer claimed that Bricco had the best crab cakes she'd ever had, pointing out that since she grew up in the Chesapeake Bay area, her standards were "very high." *Plain Dealer* reporter Debbi Snook described the service as "pleasant even under pressure."

A fire in the Hanna Building basement in January 2013 shuttered Bricco. The spot reopened in September 2013 as Cibreo Italian Kitchen, a Tuscan-themed restaurant, which was still serving Clevelanders as of August 2019.

MEMORIES

Cuisine's owner Roberta Rocco wrote:

There were many memories both good and bad. The people, our guests, were the good. My sister reminded me about two gentlemen, Hanna building tenants who would come down for Happy Hour frequently and joke with Sam about not having any "regular food" on the bar menu. Eventually Sam bought some bologna lunchmeat and would have a plate to put out for them when they arrived. Very sweet, they thought it was great! Because of our neighbor Playhouse Square, we also saw many celebrities too.

One of our most unique food offerings were food items cooked on a wood grill; we purchased a variety of woods from local people and used it in our specially built fire pit. Unfortunately it caused a severe flue fire that spread to the restaurant and closed us down. But we did have Impromptu Cuisine in the Old Arcade that we operated for a few years. The Arcade was genuine living reality theater; so many people used it for so many goods and services it was as if we were in this continual show with people moving through. We sold it to a local Korean Food Service Company.

Oh, a story about our opening Benefit party in December 1984 for Diann Scaravilli, hosting the 12th annual Back to the City [fundraiser]. However, Pam's Astrologer said we should not open then, not an astrologically good date. So we officially said our opening was in January 1985. But it didn't really matter, it still wasn't a good date or a successful opening.

The Hollenden Hotel

600 Superior and Bond/East 6th Street

The Hollenden Hotel was one of Cleveland's most important structures for many years—not just as a hotel, but as a gathering place. It's almost impossible to count how many famous restaurants were part of the hostelry over the years. It opened on June 7, 1885, was upgraded in 1926 and demolished in 1962. It was replaced by a four-hundred-room Hollenden House done in the modern Brutalist style. Before the hotel was demolished for good in 1989, it provided a roof and food for tired travelers and hungry Clevelanders.

George Francis Hammond was an architect with Koehler & Hammond. Liberty Holden commissioned him to come to Cleveland in 1885 to design the Hollenden Hotel, a luxury hostelry at Superior and Bond (East 6th) Street. When it opened, it was considered Cleveland's grandest hotel and offered rooms from one to two dollars per day. Its opening sparked the development on Short Vincent. Restaurants, entertainment venues, tailor shops, shoe repair shops, laundries, dry cleaners, barbers and watch repair shops all opened on the street because of the hotel.

The Hollenden was one of the first fire-resistant hotels in the area. Hammond oversaw much of the interior design, which was outfitted handsomely with "massive redwood and mahogany fittings," exclusively designed furniture, electric lights, one hundred private baths, a theater, a barbershop and several bars and clubs.

Liberty Holden arranged for George Myers (known as the "Best Barber in America") to operate the barbershop at the hotel. Eventually, Myers owned

Postcard of the Hollenden Hotel. *Author collection.*

the Hollenden Barber Shop. This wouldn't have been all that unusual except for the fact that Myers was African American. The future entrepreneur arrived in Cleveland in 1879. He started out at the Weddell House Barber Shop and then moved to the new Hollenden in 1888 at the request of the owner. Needless to say, the premier hotel in Cleveland didn't exactly cater to African Americans, so Myers's customers were not only primarily white, they were also "very, very influential white," like Marcus Hanna and William McKinley. It was said that Myers shaved at least eight presidents, including Cleveland, McKinley, Harrison, Hayes, Harding, Roosevelt, Taft and Wilson, along with numerous congressmen and other celebrities like David Lloyd George and Mark Twain. Obviously, this opportunity to interact with so many important Cleveland leaders, dignitaries and politicians was one of the biggest advantages Myers received from his ownership. Myers even served as a delegate to the Republican National Convention in Minneapolis,

Postcard of the Hollenden Hotel, 1910. *Author collection.*

Minnesota, in 1892. He helped get McKinley nominated for president at the 1896 Republican National Convention. He is credited with helping to secure the single vote that took Mark Hanna to the U.S. Senate in 1897— this deciding vote was cast by William H. Clifford, an African American man from Cuyahoga County.

Myers received various offers for political appointments, but he chose to focus on his barbering. The shop wasn't a one-man business either. There were about thirty-five employees. At its high point, this included seventeen barbers, three hairdressers for women, two podiatrists, six manicurists, five porters and two cashiers. Many considered his establishment to be the most modern barbershop in the country. He sold the Hollenden shop in 1930 shortly before his death.

Holden was reluctant to put in a dining room. When he finally did, the restaurant quickly became a favorite spot in Cleveland, especially with well-to-do citizens and politicians. Its elegant Crystal Room was a meeting place for politicians, and its bar was said to have been the longest in town. It was often the location of "colorful balls and festivities." The Crystal Room had ornate chandeliers under which presidents, famous singers, actors, diplomats and royalty dined. The space was enlarged in 1925.

Many dignitaries and celebrities stayed at the hotel, including five presidents: McKinley, Theodore Roosevelt, Taft, Wilson and Harding. Even Albert Einstein stayed there during his first visit to the United States in 1921. A dinner in honor of Prince Nicholas of Romania took place there in 1929, and Senator John F. Kennedy gave a speech at the hotel in 1960.

Senator Marcus Hanna was a regular at the hotel. In fact, "Hanna Hash" was his favorite, and supposedly it originated here. According to *The Breeder's Gazette: A Weekly Journal for the American Stock Farm*:

> [Corned beef was] *made famous in the form of hash by Mark Hanna, who considered it good enough to make it the chief dish at breakfast and whose hash once eaten at his table by his many guests acquired a reputation equal to that of the choicest cuts of the highest-priced meats and thus added a new luxury to the list of viands they ordered afterward at their hostelries and high-toned restaurants.*

Supposedly, people who ate Hanna's hash never ate it again except at his table because others never measured up. It's unclear if this belief affected sales at the Hollenden. In any event, apparently his hash took Washington by storm throughout the McKinley and Roosevelt administrations. So, what exactly was in the heavenly hash? Well, according to the Ladies of Saint Anselm's Church, which published the *San Anselmo Cook-Book*, the recipe was as follows:

> *Brown in a saucepan two onions with one ounce of butter; add one pound of cooked, but underdone, well chopped roast beef and one pint of mashed potatoes; moisten with any stock soup, preferably chicken broth; season with pinch of pepper, same of nutmeg; stir well, then cook for fifteen minutes; serve with poached eggs.*

Other reports suggested serving it over a fried egg. Apparently, the secret was the potatoes and onions, but *no* beets.

Other special concoctions at the hotel included its special cheese—they bored a hole in the center of the block and filled it with brandy, which permeated the whole cheese. The addition was said to give it "a piquant taste."

On New Year's Eve during the early 1900s, you could get a gin fizz for fifteen cents each or two for a quarter—a real bargain! The evening's festivities also included platters of turkey and duck served by ten additional waiters brought on to be sure the New Year got off to a good start. The waiters were as exceptional as the food at the Hollenden. They knew the proper order and accoutrements of a meal—the cocktail came before the hors d'oeuvres; sherry and oysters were a good pairing; the fish or lobster went with white Bordeaux, while red Burgundy went with the roast; a clear Rhenish wine was a good choice with game meat; sparkling champagne made dessert better; and cordials ended the repast. *Plain Dealer* reporter Roelif Loveland wrote that one New Year's festivities included

> *a steaming bowl of Tom and Jerry on the bar. A powerful mixture of various liquors topped off with cinnamon. Likewise, "compliments of the house." Help yourself. One drink and you feel good. Two, and you feel better. Three, and you hold no resentment against millionaires. Four, and you are a millionaire.*
>
> *Tomorrow you'll feel awful, because that Tom and Jerry packs a frightful headache. But tomorrow is another day and a new year.*

The Vogue Room was one of the hotel's night spots, opening just in time for the Great Lakes Exposition visitors on April 15, 1936. It featured a ten-foot-square blue mirror that had modernistic figures etched in it. Every night from 6:30 p.m. to 8:30 p.m. there was "Dinner and Dancing," and there was

"Supper Dancing" from 10:30 p.m. to 2:30 a.m., with live music. In 1952, the Vogue Room had its own entrance on Short Vincent.

During the Christmas season of 1936, the headliner at the Vogue room was magician Gali-Gali. *Plain Dealer* reviewer Glenn Pulen said that his "lightning-like hands are nearly as deft as Blackstone's in making cards and rings disappear." But it was his unusual version of the old shell game that made people really take notice. Instead of peas, he used live baby chicks. One skeptic was won over when Gali-Gali unbuttoned his coat. Surprise! Four tiny chickens nestled in the inside pocket.

In the early 1940s, Sammy Watkins, who led the orchestra at the city's top supper club, the Vogue Room, hired Dean Martin to appear with the orchestra. Martin would often dash around the corner to the Theatrical on Short Vincent to join with the jazz musicians there for an impromptu jam session. It was at this time that he took the name "Dean Martin"—he had been singing as Dino Martino before this. Not only was the Vogue Room considered the best in town, but the Sammy Watkins Orchestra was also voted "Most Popular Band in Cleveland." When the singer first started, Glen Pullen of *Variety* wrote that Martin "backs a personable kisser with a warm, low tenor and an agreeable manner." Dean pulled in thirty-five dollars per week, a free hotel room and 50 percent discount on the food at the hotel restaurant. On July 5, 1942, Dean made his first coast-to-coast radio broadcast. He and the band were featured on *The Fitch Bandwagon* on NBC broadcasting at WTAM across the street from the Hollenden. Things were going very well for the singer and the band until the very end, when the announcer, Tobe Reed, signed off with, "You've been listening to the music of Sammy Kaye and his Orchestra." Dean was the band's singer until 1943, when he went to New York, teamed up with Jerry Lewis and became one of the top entertainment acts in the country.

Harry Craddock was hired by the Hollenden in 1900 and became legendary. He wrote *The Savoy Cocktail Book*, which was published in 1930 and became the Bible for bartenders. It included the recipes for the White Lady and Corpse Reviver #2—both invented by the author. He also popularized the dry martini.

By 1963, the Hollenden was heading toward a new building, whose construction was begun even before the old one was razed. The new building was set to have four hundred rooms in fourteen stories, with a spacious lobby, a bar, dining rooms, ballrooms and meeting rooms. Probably more to the point at that moment in time, six hundred cars would be able to have their own "room" in an indoor parking garage—something the original guests couldn't even fathom.

In July 1964, when the new Hollenden's framework was completed, the developers sent out invitations for an 11:15 a.m. party on the roof. Marie Schreiber of the Tavern Chop House (who would be operating the restaurant at the hotel) was in charge of the party. Plans were made to set the tables in linen and serve the hot meal with shining silverware. However, it was suggested that those who were afraid of heights should *not* look over the side. When the day arrived, heights seemed not to be a problem, and neither was anything else. James D. Carney of the Six Hundred Superior Corporation, which was building the $6 million hotel, welcomed the group and announced the Hollenden's opening date as January 1. A bucket of concrete was hauled up, and a number of guests dug in to put a shovel full into the building's framework. And so the ground was set—or rather the roof was set—for the upcoming opening.

The Hollenden House opened in March 1965, decorated in shades of green, gold and white with touches of blues, turquoise, black and bronze. The Grand Ballroom could accommodate five hundred guests. It had a street-level coffee shop, a cocktail bar, the Gazette Lounge and the Sixth Street Lounge. The Gazette Lounge was an homage to the motif in the original Hollenden. The coffee shop was done in pink, orange, lavender and white. The Intimate Angel Club for men was on the second level.

The main dining room was to be called the Tavern Restaurant. Food service was to be managed by Marie Schreiber. The night manager was Herman Pirchner, formerly of the Alpine Village. The hotel was designed to have a club atmosphere with the "personalized comfort and service of a well-run private club."

Schreiber, the owner/operator of the Tavern Chop House on Chester Avenue, was best known as the "charming and fashionably dressed proprietor of The Tavern." She came to the Hollenden when the original Tavern closed. When she went to the Hollenden, the customers asked if the "new" Tavern would be like the old one. Schreiber said that the question sort of dared her "to have it any other way." The new Hollenden Tavern, which could seat two hundred, was basically the same. The food was identical, although the décor was changed. The rustic wood feeling was retained with wood paneling. The room was done in blue, red and gold, with a specially designed carpet with a blue background and gold English medallions. Benches were red nylon with tufted backs and matching leather seats. Walls were covered with a soft gold felt for acoustical qualities. There were brass fixtures and a leaded, stained-glass door covering the wine rack.

Marie Schreiber operated the Hollenden Tavern until 1971.

The Gazette Room eventually became a "stag" place. On April 22, 1972, attorney Jean Capers and Rosemarie Folkman demanded lunch there. Capers was a local lawyer for the National Organization for Women and was the first African American woman elected to Cleveland City Council. The managers responded by getting free beers for Capers and Folkman, thus ending the "stag" era there.

The Hollenden House closed in May 1989 after struggling with poor economic conditions in Cleveland during the 1980s. It was demolished and became the site of a new bank building.

In the "strange but true" category, one of the city's most bizarre events happened at the Hollenden. It was so strange that it received national recognition from the *New York Times*. In March 1905, a New Yorker named Henry L. Woodward and a traveling salesman from Toledo, Ohio, named Charles A. Brouse both committed suicide by shooting themselves during the night at the hotel. This was extremely peculiar because these men did not know each other, yet they both died in the same manner during the night at the same hotel. There was no evidence presented to connect or link these two deaths. As a final curiosity in the deathly duet, the revolvers involved were of the same caliber.

Hornblower's Barge & Grille

1151 North Marginal Road

Hornblower's was part of the Pufferbelly Restaurant chain and was named Hornblower's Barge and Grill after the dashing sea captain Horatio Hornblower, made famous in the novels written by T.S. Forester in the 1930s and '40s. The restaurant was constructed on the deck of the aft end of the lake freighter *Kearsarge*, built in 1894. It was designed to have all utilities supplied via flexible connections from shore. Located at the west end of Burke Lakefront Airport and east of the SS *Cod* submarine museum, Hornblower's opened on the 100th anniversary of the christening of the original hull of the *Kearsarge*.

Owned by Tom Roehl and partner George Lewis, the unique restaurant opened in September 1992. The pair decided that they wanted a floating restaurant, so they went looking for a barge. Their first visit to Dunbar & Sullivan Dredging gave them pause. They found a barge—a really *big* one. A little daunted by its size, the pair left to think it over. Deciding that it was sink or swim, they went back to claim it, only to find that it had already been sold. Not to worry. They were informed that there was another one available at Stoney Island in Detroit. Off they went to look it over. This one was 150 feet long and in very bad shape. They hired an inspector, who told them that although it was ugly, it would float just fine.

Taking a chance that they could solve the "ugly problem," they had it towed back to Sandusky to turn it into a "beautiful barge." It was no easy task, but they did it. Then there was the minor problem of getting it from Sandusky to Cleveland. They "set sail" on July 11, 1992, for Cleveland's

MAIN DINING ROOM PARTITIONS —
SOME WOODWORK INSTALLED

BAR (UPSTAIRS) TAKING SHAPE

Hornblower's Restaurant interior, under construction. *Courtesy of Tom Roehl.*

Hornblower's Restaurant. *Courtesy of Tom Roehl.*

Inner Harbor under tow of the tug *Little Toot*. An hour later, they were stuck on a sandbar, and the aptly named big tug *Superior* came to the rescue. Eventually, they made it up to thirteen knots as they headed east. Arriving in Cleveland after dark (or "sneaking in," as Tom Roehl described it), they were met by a group of well-wishers. But the excitement wasn't over yet. Would they clear the SS *Cod*? They made it…by eight feet.

By September 1992, the ugly duckling was now grown up and beautiful. Flags, awnings and signs were up, and Hornblower's was open for business. On September 17, Cleveland mayor Mike White stood on the top deck of the restaurant and declared it "Hornblower's Day" in honor of the 100th anniversary of the original christening of the barge hull.

No prepared foods were used in the menu items, although some things like seafood were fresh-frozen. Fish and seafood were the specialty, served both indoors and outdoors. A jazz combo played on the upper deck with a great view of the city. *Crain's Cleveland Business* called it one of the city's "memorable places," not only for its food but also because it was one of the few places to eat, drink and watch the sun set over the lake.

Like any other show, there was plenty of backstage drama. Sump pumps had to be installed in the hull of the barge to handle the water needs of the restaurant. There was a backup system, but the system handled *all* the drains, including the toilets, so when it failed, it was an immediate crisis.

The water level in the lake was also a problem. Getting the boarding and service ramps designed properly was difficult. They had to be able to accommodate the water level's constant changing and the back-and-forth movement of the boat alongside the dock. The lake could be so erratic that sometimes the bridges would fail, and then people would have to enter via the service ramp through the kitchen, giving customers a backstage tour the management hadn't planned.

Of course, then there was the one never-ending problem none of the employees wanted to deal with: flotsam floating by the entryways.

When Roehl retired around 2006, the restaurant closed, but the building continued housing businesses until 2011, when LeanDog Software Company and the Arras Group moved in. As of 2020, they continue to offer a menu of custom software and business consulting in this unusual structure.

Il Giardino d'Italia
(Chef Hector Boiardi)

There might not be a more recognizable name for kids and spaghetti than Chef Boy-Ar-Dee. Everyone knows his smiling face on all those cans. But Chef Hector was not only a real person, he was a real chef, and his career started in Cleveland. He was a groundbreaking chef, a visionary businessman and a savvy restaurateur who became a leader and multimillionaire in the packaged foods industry. His nephew, Paul Boiardi, remembered him as "the most elegant gentleman I ever met in my life. He'd become a nervous wreck if you ever caught him without a tie."

Ettore Boiardi was born in the village of Piacenza, Italy, on October 22, 1897. Legend has it that his first baby rattle was a wire whisk. Early on, he found his love of cooking as an assistant in one of the local restaurants, La Croce Bianca, which hired him when he was eleven years old. In 1914, he braved the long ocean voyage and arrived at Ellis Island, where he became known as Hector.

Hector joined his brother Paolo, who was the maître d' of the Plaza Hotel in New York City. His brother helped to get Hector a job in the hotel kitchen. Soon, Hector worked his way up to head chef. His quick rise to success continued when, at the age of eighteen, he was hired to cater Woodrow Wilson's wedding to Edith Bolling Galt on December 18, 1915, at the Greenbrier Hotel in West Virginia. Apparently, the president was happy with his wedding feast because he chose Boiardi to supervise the preparation of the homecoming meal that President Wilson held at the White House for two thousand returning World War I soldiers.

Cleveland hoteliers decided that they needed this celebrity chef to come to town, and they wasted no time in wooing him to the North Coast. Hector's first job was at the Hotel Winton, on Prospect Avenue, in 1917. He commanded the kitchen and created a sensation with his exotic spaghetti dinners, a thrilling change from Clevelanders' usual fare.

Boiardi opened his first restaurant, Il Giardino d'Italia (The Garden of Italy), in 1924 at East 9th and Woodland. Like his other culinary ventures, his new place was a hit with the locals and visiting celebrities. It was said to be "the meeting ground for all the Metropolitan Opera singers and maestros" during the 1920s and '30s. "When they were here, they wouldn't go anywhere else," son Mario said.

Soon people started requesting jars full of Boiardi's special pasta sauce to take home. It all started when customers began asking for the recipe, but he wasn't quite so willing to share the secrets to the sauce, so Chef Hector would fill empty milk bottles for his customers. Although his customers took the sauce home, they would often return, complaining that it didn't taste the same when they made it. The chef told them they were using the wrong pasta. A friend told Hector that rather than trying to "coach the clueless," he should just offer the whole meal to go. Soon he was charging for packages of uncooked pasta, cheese and bottles of sauce, and the income from this side business began to exceed the restaurant's. Basically, he invented carryout meals.

The carryout business was so successful that he and his brothers, Paul and Mario, started the Chef Boiardi Food Company in 1928 and built a small factory.

Not long afterward, Chef Hector was approached by Maurice and Eva Wiener. They saw a real opportunity behind Boiardi's home-cooked Italian food. What's more, they owned a grocery store franchise. Their idea was to have the chef put his pasta sauce in cans and sell them nationwide. The three of them developed a canning process, and by 1929, they had introduced the pasta to the public. The release was such a big success that they needed to make a swift and massive expansion of the chef's products.

Boiardi used only natural and homegrown ingredients, and he needed more space to grow the mushrooms, tomatoes and other produce for the sauce. So the factory was moved from Cleveland to Milton, Pennsylvania. The other big change that came about with the move was that they changed the spelling of his name to "Boyardee" to make sure everyone could say his name correctly.

At the time, Italian food was considered new and fashionable. It was an inexpensive way to feed the entire family. Things like spaghetti and meatballs had emerged from the isolation of Italian neighborhoods in large cities to take a solid place in American culinary culture. The sauce and pasta were easy to mass-produce, and at a time when most Americans didn't have much money, they could be sold at reasonable prices. This first prepackaged meal (1928) contained a bundle of dry spaghetti, a packet with grated Parmesan cheese and spaghetti sauce in a milk bottle. It sold for sixty cents and could feed a family of four.

During World War II, Boiardi provided these packaged meals to soldiers overseas and was eventually awarded the Gold Star Award for Excellence from the U.S. War Department.

By the 1950s, the business was expanding internationally, and Boiardi couldn't keep up with the management, so he sold the brand to American Home Foods (now International Home Goods). Although he originally fought the idea, it turned out to be a good one for both him and American Home Foods, which asked him to become the "face of the brand"—that picture on the can really is Chef Boiardi.

In spite of the success of his canned food business, the chef never got out of the restaurant business. In 1931, he opened Chef Boiardi's at 823 Prospect Avenue. The name was later changed to Chef Hector's, and it closed in 1967. In 1945, he and Albert Caminati operated Pierre's Italian Restaurant at 1524 Euclid Avenue. It closed in 1974. They opened Town & Country Restaurant on Chagrin Boulevard in the 1950s.

Hector Boiardi died of natural causes on June 21, 1985, in Parma, Ohio, and is buried at All Souls Cemetery in Chardon. At one time, he was described by the chancellor of Italy as "the world's greatest chef." A spokesperson for the James Beard Foundation called him "one of Cleveland's most recognizable contributions to the food world." Chef Hector Boiardi was posthumously inducted into the Foundation's Culinary Hall of Fame in 1995.

MEMORIES

On June 25, 2018, Peggie Brown remembered "going to Chef Hector's as a teenager or young adult with my mother and her 'lady friends.' One of her friends was the sister of Chef Boyardee—Hector Boiardi. All the workers would say hello to all of us; we felt very special."

The Mayfair Casino

1511 Euclid Avenue

During the Depression, the availability of Broadway shows became so limited that the Ohio Theatre on Euclid Avenue remained dark for many months. By October 24, 1934, it had closed. Not quite a year later, on October 22, 1935, the theater reopened as the Mayfair Casino. The new nightclub targeted the "top hat and formal gown crowd."

The Mayfair was called "Cleveland's Million Dollar Theatre Restaurant," according to a postcard issued at the time. It went on to give this glowing description: "The Mayfair Casino in Cleveland, Ohio is a theatre restaurant so intriguing so perfect in its appointments and subtle good taste so superlative in its service so ultra-modern different and new it will entice you to come again and again." The cocktail lounge area in the theater lobby was described as the "Largest and most beautiful Cocktail Lounge in America." The circular bar in the lounge was said to be the longest in the world. On the old balcony level, there was a "sky bar," which offered Champagne cocktails at seventy-five cents.

The theater auditorium was remodeled and had a circular stage, a bar and dinner tables. The kitchen was put in under the old stage.

The Mayfair had 16 bartenders and 112 servers to cater to its customers. Dinner ran from 5:30 p.m. to 10:00 p.m., and supper was from 10:00 p.m. to closing. Although most meals cost $1.50, the filet mignon ran $2.25. There was a good wine list with selections of Bordeaux, Burgundies, Champagnes, sherries and ports from Italy, Hungary and California. A 1920 vintage

Postcard of the interior of the Mayfair Casino. *Courtesy of Alan Dutka.*

Dancing at the Mayfair Casino. *Courtesy of Alan Dutka.*

Hungarian wine sold for $6.00, and the most expensive bottle of Champagne (a 1926 Pol Roger) cost $12.00.

Along with the top-notch food and drink offerings, customers could dance to the music of the nation's top orchestras. The Casino had three dance bands to provide entertainment with no cover charge. A two-hour stage show cost one dollar. The show played to an audience of 864 patrons in a portion of the Ohio Theatre's auditorium and balcony. Show times were 7:30 p.m. and 11:30 p.m. and included the most popular entertainers of the day—Tommy Dorsey, Sophie Tucker, Noble Sissle, Xavier Cugat and many others. On New Year's Eve 1936, the six-dollar cover charge allowed revelers to enjoy Red Nichols and His Five Pennies.

In July 1937, the Casino was planning a new sidewalk café that *Plain Dealer* reporter Glen Pullen said would make it "one of Euclid Avenue's smartest and most colorful spots." A new bar in the foyer would be surrounded by tables and palm trees extending into the lobby. A "miniature bandstand" was being built for a new girls' ensemble that would double with Fred Heikel's Gypsies. Pullen concluded that these changes would "give Cleveland the nearest thing to the St. Moritz Hotel's sidewalk café in New York."

Unfortunately, the planned changes didn't change the fate of the restaurant. The Mayfair only lasted two years and had financial difficulties from the start. In fact, during the summer of 1936, the Casino closed everything except the cocktail lounge. By December, it had declared bankruptcy. It reopened on Christmas Day under Durries "Duke" Crane, who converted the lobby into a sidewalk café.

Harry Proper was nominally in charge of running the casino. He was apparently the front man for the Syndicate, which actually owned the Casino. Its "members" included Moe Dalitz, Morris Klienman, Sam Tucker and Lou Rothkopf, who was part of the notorious Mayfield Road Gang, "which had the local monopoly on vice, gambling and bootlegging." Other silent partners included the city's Mafia representatives, the Polizzi brothers.

Financial problems continued, and the Mayfair Casino closed permanently on November 25, 1937.

Mills Restaurants

315–319 Euclid Avenue

James Owen Mills was president of the Mills Restaurant Company, which had operations in Cleveland, Columbus and Cincinnati. He was born in Marysville, Ohio, on September 18, 1883, and studied at Lima Business College, Lima, Ohio. In 1902, he began working in restaurants in Columbus. Eventually, he opened his own business—a self-service-style restaurant that was quite novel for the times. His operations were efficient and planned out on a larger scale than others. In a short time, his eateries were considered a class apart.

James opened the first Mills Restaurant in Columbus in 1911. Because it was a self-service restaurant, it was considered an oddity. Apparently, the customers didn't mind because over the next five years he opened five more restaurants in Columbus, Cincinnati and Cleveland.

The Cleveland Mills Restaurant was founded in 1919 at 315–319 Euclid Avenue. The restaurant was located in a new building built especially for Mills. It had a windmill logo with a sign that read, "Stop at the sign of Mill's mill." The restaurant could seat 650 people.

When the site opened on April 23, 1919, James Mills entertained his friends with an inspection of his latest restaurant followed by a "dinner at the Hotel Hollenden." However, this appeared not to be an indictment of the food at his place.

This new Mills Restaurant was the first in the country to have three service counters and one of the first cafeteria-style eateries. It boasted main floor, mezzanine and basement dining rooms. The first floor had marble wainscoting

Postcard of the Mills Restaurant. *Courtesy of Alan Dutka.*

all around with mirrors above it. Tile floors were placed throughout the dining area, as well as in the kitchen, pantries and bakeries, with other rooms having cement floors. It had its own refrigeration plant with a twelve-ton capacity. Employees had four separate locker rooms, two with shower baths.

Its most popular entrées were prime rib and fried chicken, while the strawberry shortcake headed the dessert list. It was remodeled in 1930 and closed in 1970 when it was absorbed by the Women's Federal Building.

MEMORIES

Dodi Lettus remembered on September 10, 2018, that her first date was at Mills Restaurant with the windmill sign.

New York Spaghetti House

2173 East 9th Street

Mario and Maria Brigotti opened the New York Spaghetti House in 1927, and it became the longest-running family-operated restaurant in Cleveland. Mario patterned the eatery after the basement spaghetti house he had worked in while living in New York. Mario's brother, Marino, left Rome to come to work at the restaurant in the late 1940s. He eventually became head chef, retiring in 1985. Big bowls of spaghetti covered with the Spaghetti House's signature "brown sauce" was the specialty. Mario's son James took over the restaurant in the 1950s and remained in charge until it closed in January 2001.

The building was built in 1870 as the parsonage of Zion Lutheran Church. In 1904, the Lyric Theatre bought the church. The old parsonage was used to house its actors. In 1921, it became the New Empire Theatre and replaced the Empire Theatre on Huron. When the restaurant bought the parsonage, the theater supplied the restaurant with some regular customers, including Red Skelton, W.C. Fields, Jimmy Durante and Mickey Rooney. Often the performers would stay upstairs in the restaurant when other housing wasn't available.

In spite of its name, the Spaghetti House catered to its Turkish and Greek neighbors by providing a Turkish coffeehouse atmosphere where customers drank Turkish coffee and smoked Turkish cigarettes and hookahs.

The New York Spaghetti House provided not just a dining experience, but an *artistic* experience. Mario commissioned Art Deco still life pieces for the lower dining room in the 1930s. They were replaced with murals

Exterior of the New York Spaghetti House, 1994. *Photo by author.*

by John Cgosz in 1956. These later pictures were commissioned by James Brigotti, and they depicted scenes from Italy, including Venetian gondoliers, the island of Capri, Rome's Coliseum and scenes from Florence and Capri. The wood-paneled walls and red-and-white checked tablecloths were a perfect complement to these paintings and helped with the "old country" feel. James Brigotti's wife, Patricia, created a respected art gallery in 1987 in a renovated dining room upstairs.

The New York Spaghetti House closed in 2001. It reopened for a short time in 2004. R. House Inc. bought the building in 2014. The building was torn down in 2015 and replaced with a parking lot.

MEMORIES

On May 3 and October 29, 2018, Linda Heiden provided some special memories of the New York Spaghetti House:

When I was getting married in 1974, my bachelorette party was at the New York Spaghetti House (by default). Because we were young and dressed in the fashion of the time (bell-bottom jeans and halter tops) they would not let us into the Kon-Tiki, which is where we were supposed to dine. [At the party, the ladies got a somewhat more unique presentation of their order than they were expecting. Linda wrote that there were] *all male waiters at the New York Spaghetti House…and also you might remember that they never wrote an order down—they proudly did it all from memory and didn't make any mistakes either. Their claim to*

Above: Linda Heiden and her server, who brought her the risqué plate of spaghetti. *Courtesy of Linda Heiden.*

Opposite: Linda Heiden's bachelorette party at the New York Spaghetti House in 1974. *Courtesy of Linda Heiden.*

fame was their delicious "brown" meat sauce, and I'm sure that is what I ordered, because that was my usual....Delicious! Anyway, when my plate arrived 44 years ago, arranged just so on top were two meatballs with a long piece of Italian sausage between them—pretty risqué!! If you know what I mean. I guess since we were very young and innocent, we didn't want to take a photo of that (not like these days), so we must have taken a photo of me with their sparkler-decorated dessert instead but were still laughing from receiving the entrées!

...I also remember going there with my parents when I was younger and also going there with my new husband and daughter and other family members over the years. Sometimes, when we were in downtown Cleveland, we'd just stop in and order a quart of their wonderful spaghetti sauce to take home.

Jim Higgins wrote on September 10, 2018, "They had great spaghetti, my wife and I went there shortly after our wedding. We were seated on the main floor and shortly after being served the waiter came over and politely said to my wife 'we do not cut our spaghetti here,' to which my wife responded, 'I'm from Baltimore and we cut our spaghetti.'"

Marian Macbeth recalled on August 10, 2018, "Our go-to before going to the Palace or Severance Hall was the Spaghetti House on East 9th. My favorite was the pesto sauce on angel hair pasta & a caprese salad. Loved the maître d. He was so elegant."

Old Allen Theatre Restaurant

1501 Euclid Avenue

The Allen Theatre got a $500,000 makeover in 1977, with the Old Allen Theatre Restaurant reopening in the lobby and rotunda area. It was not a dinner theater—it was dinner *in* a theater. Weldon A. Carpenter was scheduled to be "chief chef." Carpenter said of his new job, "I feel like a kid with a new toy. I have been given all the freedom I want, to prepare the dishes I want and I will have only quality products to work with." He was happy to have the opportunity to combine his love of food preparation with his love of theater in this new offering in Playhouse Square. Previously, he worked for the Rusty Scupper while volunteering at Playhouse Square as historian. In 1975, Carpenter was named one of the five top chefs in the nation by *Gourmet* magazine. More recently, the chef had made a home in the Playhouse Square Theatres (literally) as he worked with Ray Shephardson to bring the entertainment complex back to life. At one time, he was personal chef to Judy Garland in Hyannis Port, Massachusetts—a perfect background for a chef in a restaurant in a theater!

The Allen Theatre opened on April 1, 1921, and its rotunda provided a unique location for diners in this otherworldly space designed in Renaissance style.

The Old Allen and the Lobby were not the first eating establishments in the theater. In 1922, there was a soda fountain called the Tea Room on the main floor open to the auditorium. Although this restaurant was only available to theater ticketholders, it allowed the theatergoers to drink sodas as they watched the movies—although that's a rather simplistic description of this eatery. The Tea Room contained "every imaginable form of soft drink and ice cream dish" in a "soft and harmonious setting." The room had about seventy tables, and about half were able to view the screen from there. The small table lights were set low so as not to interfere with the screening. The lampshades were in soft colors. Persian rugs covered the floor in mild color combinations. Because the theater acoustics were so perfect, the audience in the Tea Room could hear as well as the patrons in the auditorium. When singer/actress Eva Tanguay appeared at the theater, Tea Room manager T.B. Lanahan created an "Eva Tanguay Special" sundae. The fountain room regularly created an atmosphere that complemented the shows. For *The Sheik*, they decorated as the "Land of the Sheiks," while the theater ushers were dressed in silks and satins. Besides the desert atmosphere, Lanahan made a new sundae called the "Arabian Special."

These festivities in the Tea Room did not come easily. During the construction of the theater, the owners had to petition for approval to install the fountain because the carbonic gas drums used in the fountain could explode. However, designer C. Howard Crane explained that the tanks would be kept in the kitchen so they would not pose a danger to the audience.

Manager Lanahan, who had previously worked as fountain manager of the Crane Candy Company at Euclid and East 12th Street (yes, the company that invented Life Savers candy), planned to begin serving lunch in the Tea Room for matinee attendees and catering services for afternoon tea parties. The fountain service would run from 11:30 a.m. until 6:00 p.m. The Tea Room gained a reputation for spotlessness, attentive and courteous waiters and special dishes. Its fame grew to the point that out-of-town guests made a point to visit. Because no other theaters were offering fountain or lunch service in their facilities, it put the Allen in a class by itself.

The Old Allen closed in 1979 and became the Lobby Restaurant from 1980 to 1982. Today, the Allen Theatre is just that—a theater.

Otto Moser's

2042–2044 Sheriff Street, 1425 Euclid Avenue

Otto Moser's Café in the Krause Building at 2042–2044 Sheriff Street (now East 4th Street) was best known for its popularity with Cleveland's theatrical crowd. It was basically Cleveland's version of New York's Sardi's.

The Krause Building was built in 1912/13 by William and Charles Krause in the heart of the city's theater district. The Krauses were longtime theatrical and masquerade costumers, and the building housed their store, office and tailor shop on the second and third floors. For fifty years, Otto Moser's Café, on the ground floor, was a favorite meeting place of the actors and actresses performing in the eight nearby theaters, including the Euclid Avenue Opera House, the Star Theatre, the White Elephant, the Prospect and the Hippodrome.

Otto Moser opened his tavern in 1893, and it represented a genuine German *wirtschaft* (a saloon or café in this context). It opened right after the Euclid Avenue Opera House reopened after a fire, and it quickly became *the* place to be. Moser's was in direct competition with Julius Deursch's Drugstore, which had a soda fountain where, in spite of the name, Fred Gillen served up cocktails "in genteel teacups for female matinee-goers." Besides the drugstore, the Opera House offered competition with its turkey and fried oyster sandwiches at the bar.

Because of its convenient location across from the Opera House, actors and musicians would come over to Otto Moser's during intermissions to get a quick drink or snack, often "breaking into libation-induced performances

Wonder Bar sign next to the door to what was originally Krause Costume, 2019. *Photo by author.*

and sing-alongs." The theater patrons would use a tunnel beneath 4th Street to go to the downstairs entrance of the restaurant.

Since women did not frequent public bars in the 1890s, the ladies would go to the private club in the basement called the Cheese Cellar, and the men would go upstairs. The "Cheese Club"—a group of theater aficionados—began meeting there in 1896. They would gather around a table with a huge wheel of cheese on it. Many of the actors and actresses from the Opera House would visit and do private shows for the guests. These club actors included George M. Cohan, Eddie Foy, Lillian Russell, Lew Dockstader and Cleveland society people, politicians and journalists. In the 1920s, the Cheese Cellar became a haven for chess tournaments.

Otto Moser's reputation was made when the theater stars started dropping in between acts and leaving autographed pictures, which were displayed in cases opposite the stunning fifty-two-foot bar. The pictures piled up, but in spite of that, it was said that Otto could find any picture in any case—C.W. Couldock, Blanche Ring, William Farnum, John Philip Sousa, Fanny Brice, Edwin Booth and Gertrude Lawrence. Will Rogers left his picture

Original exterior of Otto Moser's. *Courtesy of Alan Dutka.*

and threatened to "shoot the place full of holes" if he came back to the restaurant and could not find his picture in the case.

Besides the pictures of stars, Otto had another "celebrity" on his wall: the head of a moose named Bullwinkle. If a bride came to the restaurant on her wedding day, she was supposed to climb on the bar and give Bullwinkle a kiss. The moose collected a lot of kisses and eventually lost his left ear, which fell into a customer's bowl of soup. Presumably, the ear did not fall off due to too many kisses!

Moser suffered major setbacks when the Euclid Avenue Opera House was torn down in 1922, during Prohibition and when the theater district moved to Playhouse Square. At the restaurant, though, the "show" went on. Otto was part of the ambiance of the establishment in a striped shirt, suspenders and bowtie. He served beer and corned beef sandwiches and was known for his German potato salad and ham sandwiches. For many years, Otto smoked his own ham in the basement of the restaurant in large barrels. Moser stuck around long enough to see Prohibition repealed and survived.

After Otto retired, other proprietors kept the place running. Customers enjoyed the display cases of long-ago stars and were amazed to find out that the now run-down street had once been home to the city's most opulent theater. One man came to eat and found his mother looking back at him from a picture behind one of the glass cases. However, the restaurant remained largely unchanged until Otto's death in 1942.

Max A. and Max B. Joseph took over ownership in the 1950s and '60s, and they made some minor changes, including a new terrazzo floor that replaced the sawdust-covered red brick and a new mahogany bar. What never changed were the corned beef and the German potato salad. The strong ties between the restaurant and show business celebrities remained as well. The eatery often closed its doors to the public so that performers from the Metropolitan Opera could have the place to themselves. They even opened a second location in Cleveland's Park Center for a short time in the mid-1970s. Dan Dir and Steve Dimotsis purchased Moser's in 1977.

In February 1994, Dir and Dimotsis packed up all the display cases, 1,200 autographed pictures and six mounted animal heads (including Bullwinkle) and moved them all to a new location in Playhouse Square at 1425 Euclid Avenue in the Bulkley Building. The new spot was two and a half times bigger than the original location and could seat 135 (including bar seating). The move also included Norma Bunner, a waitress who had come to work at the restaurant in 1955.

In true theatrical style, Moser's was the location of the city's loudest St. Patrick's Day cheer of 1994. Shortly after the end of the parade at 2:45 p.m., owner Steve Dimostsis pulled up in front of Moser's new spot and waved a piece of paper over his head. The spectators cheered, whistled and applauded as if they were looking at a hard-won trophy. What all the

Otto Moser. *Courtesy of Alan Dutka.*

excitement was about was Otto Moser's new liquor license—just in time to serve the first beer at its new location on what could arguably be called "the biggest drinking day of the year" in Cleveland.

Many thought that it was the wrong time to leave East 4th since the new Jacobs Field was about to pump new life into the 4th Street District, but how many of those baseball fans would know (or care) about Al Jolson, Fanny

Above: Interior of Otto Moser's at Playhouse Square, 2018. *Photo by author.*

Left: The Republic Food and Drink's wall in honor of Otto Moser's, 2019. *Photo by author.*

Exterior of the Republic Food and Drink at the Otto Moser site at Playhouse Square, 2019. *Photo by author.*

Brice or Gertrude Lawrence or any of the other hundreds of stage stars gracing the walls? Otto Moser's moved into the new heart of the theater district to continue its long Cleveland tradition. Unfortunately, the tradition stopped in September 2018, when it finally closed for good.

However, when Republic Food and Drink moved into the vacated space, it wanted to retain the theatrical/historical ambiance. It was allowed to scan some of the pictures from the original collection, and these new versions now adorn the walls of the new restaurant. The original pictures are currently at the Cleveland State University Library, Special Collections.

Back at the old location on East 4th Street, the Wonder Bar has taken residence in the spot.

The original Otto Moser's is now home to the Wonder Bar, 2019. *Photo by author.*

MEMORIES

Lynette Filips remembered on October 29, 2018: "I don't think that many people knew that such a cool, historic place could be a stone's throw from the pawn shops and prostitutes of the 1970s Prospect Avenue we all knew. A co-worker from CEI introduced me to the establishment, and at his suggestion I ordered a corned beef sandwich, which was scrumptious."

Pewter Mug

207 Frankfort Avenue

The Pewter Mug was once described as "a mid-priced mecca for high-powered customers."

Founded by Bob Wertheim with Al Bernstein and Herb Hambourger in 1962, the Mug was decorated as an English pub with wood paneling, as well as scenes from England with photos of Plymouth Harbor, the *Mayflower* and Buckland Abbey that were provided by the British Consul. Honey-dipped chicken, ribeye steaks, julienned salads and other treats were dished up in the kitchen. At the bar were mugs with the names of the regular customers on them.

The Mug wasn't some staid place to eat in spite of its celebrity customers. Owner Bob Wertheim (who owned a number of restaurants in his career) popularized onion rings and silly jokes, and the room was filled with gossip, debate and banter.

Table 14 was *the table* and was often occupied by notables like George Steinbrenner and Art Modell. It was the place where deals and careers were made—or not. The famous Formica-topped table was the outside-of-the-office office for many Cleveland businessmen. Although the group gatherings at Table 14 included frivolity and high spirits among the various developers, lawyers, policemen, judges and journalists, there was plenty of work being done too. To prove that they meant business even in this informal setting, there was a phone at the table so they could be reached there. Like any other gathering of top dogs, there were tussles over who would get the check. The ones between George Steinbrenner and Art Model were legendary.

Postcard of the interior of the Pewter Mug at Frankfort. *Courtesy of Alan Dutka.*

Journalist Michael D. Roberts once wrote, "At its zenith, Table 14 was more informative than the City Club, more interesting than the six o'clock news, and more relevant than either. Out-of-town reporters would visit and write about the table. For a time, it was, other than the orchestra, the only bright spot in town."

When the items in the Frankfort Avenue site were sold off at auction because the building was being torn down for the Ameritrust Center, Table 14 was one of the first items to be sold.

The flagship location on Frankfort closed on April 28, 1990. City hall marked the occasion by calling the event "Remember the Mug Day." But the Mug wasn't empty just yet. It filled in empty spaces around the city with many area franchises over the years.

One Pewter Mug opened in 1979 in the Citizens Building on Euclid Avenue near East 9th Street and was managed by Bob Stiner. Similar in décor and atmosphere to the original, this one also had a see-through fireplace that led into one of four spacious rooms for leisurely lunching. Yet another Pewter Mug showed up at the Hanna Building in Playhouse Square in 1965 under the ownership of John Cardullias. Eventually, more Mugs showed up in outlying areas like Mentor, Akron, Columbus and more.

MEMORIES

Lynette Filips remembered on October 29, 2018: "A short, narrow street—Frankfurt [*sic*], maybe—ran west off Public Square in front of part of the Illuminating Company building. On it was a restaurant called The Pewter Mug. It was part of the Pewter Mug chain, and was where we girls would most often go when we wanted to eat lunch out. Their meals came with a salad with the Pewter Mug's signature creamy garlic dressing, and frugal customers like we were knew that we could also just order a salad separately."

Sheriff Street/4ᵗʰ Street

The Place to Meet and Eat

4ᵗʰ Street was one of the early twentieth-century hot spots, just as it is in 2019. Prior to its renaissance in the early 2000s, its most famous eatery was Otto Moser's. However, there were many other popular places along this short stretch of street. The Euclid Avenue Opera House at the southeast corner of East 4ᵗʰ Street and Euclid Avenue provided the impetus for the opening of many restaurants on this street, including Jimmy McGlade's 4ᵗʰ Street Restaurant, Café Windsor (which opened in 1876 and combined an ice cream parlor with Whitman's candies, flowers and cigars), the Opera House Café (which only served men while women stayed in their seats and ate chocolate), Billiard Power (which advertised the best liquors, lager beer and Havana cigars), Schlitz's Atlas Beer Tavern, the Rathskeller and, of course, Otto Moser's.

The Feichtmeier family operated a restaurant on the street from 1910 to 1917 (address unknown) and then in 1918 moved to 2230 East 4ᵗʰ, where they stayed for twenty-four years (as the Feichtmeier Restaurant). The Daisy Café took over that space in 1942, offering a business lunch of soup and beer for twenty-four cents; however, it only lasted a year.

Cleveland's first Cotton Club borrowed the name of that famous Harlem jazz spot. Opened in 1934 at 2226 East 55ᵗʰ Street, it was owned by Bernie Berstein and featured such early bands as the Don Redman Orchestra and Fletcher Henderson's All-Star New York Review featuring Dewey Washington, Eunice Wilson, Mabel Scott, the Three Brown Bears, mime Johnny Hudgins and Two Piano Queens. Even though the shows

Postcard of the Rathskeller. *Courtesy of Alan Dutka.*

were successful enough to be extended, that first Cotton Club on 55th did not last very long.

In 1954, when Sam Firsten opened his Cotton Club nightclub at 2230 East 4th Street, at the corner of 4th and Huron (near today's Quicken Loans Arena), he started a parade of jazz greats marching through the city. Opening night featured the Jimmy Saunders Band with saxophonists Joe Alexander and Paul Redfron, bassist Rodney Richardson and drummer Lawrence Jackson. Soon the show was being emceed by Cleveland singer Jimmy Scott. Within a year, Firsten began booking national big-name jazz artists. The club presented many of the most important musicians in jazz at the time, all playing seven nights a week from 9:30 p.m. until 3:30 a.m. Some of the musicians who played the club during this time included trumpeter Ruby Braff and his quintet, the Matt Matthews Jazz Quartet featuring flutist Herbie Mann, Gene Ammons ("Mr. Mighty of the Cool Sax") and His Quintet, saxophonist Arthur Prysock and the Duke Ellington Orchestra. There was entertainment seven nights a week with matinees on Sundays, and there was a downstairs cocktail lounge that was open on Friday and Saturday nights.

Around 1957, the Cotton Club, renamed the Modern Jazz Room, kept alive the tradition of featuring some of the biggest names in jazz, including Erroll Garner, Miles Davis, George Shearing and Dizzy Gillespie. When Carmen McRae sang at the club, it was reported that "you could hear a pin drop. She could mesmerize an audience." McRae wasn't the only singer to hold court there—in 1957, Billie Holiday played there too.

Firsten continued to book big-name jazz stars, but increasing salary demands got the better of him. He sold the club to Fats Heard and Dr. Jim Bard in 1959. Heard was a drummer who had toured with Lionel Hampton and Erroll Garner. He was the featured drummer on Erroll Garner's classic recording of "Misty," which gave him legendary status. Some 250 people attended the November 2 opening, including football players Jim Brown and Willie Davis and future mayor Carl Stokes. In spite of Heard's legendary drummer standing, the ambiance of the club was anything but legendary (or even classic). It mainly consisted of chrome and plastic chairs, with tables only big enough to hold four cocktail glasses—basically a "mixture of dingy and tacky," as author Alan Dutka put it. Despite this lack of elegance, it did not lack in entertainment, which was provided by such jazz virtuosos as Count Basie, Duke Ellington, Sarah Vaughan, Dave Brubeck, Billie Holiday and, of course, Erroll Garner. Performer pay hikes eventually shut down the club, which could no longer turn a profit.

After Heard sold the club around 1960, it became Club Downbeat, which featured local jazz artists such as Bobby Few and Lawrence "Jacktown" Jackson and national stars such as Gloria Lynne of the Harry Belafonte Spectacular. Trouble came to the club in August 1961 when a padlock order was issued due to a charge of prostitution.

The Persian Lounge moved into the site for a brief period, ending the run of the jazz parade. From Persia, the place went to Greece. George Koropoulis purchased it and in 1963 turned it into the Grecian Gardens, complete with belly dancers.

The Grecian Gardens served both Greek and American cuisine. It was a popular lunch spot but is most remembered for the authentic Greek artists who performed during the dinner shows at 8:30 p.m. and at the 11:30 p.m. and 1:00 a.m. supper shows. Artists and musicians found an appreciative audience in Clevelanders, but the exotic belly dancers of the shows quickly became the fan favorites. Visiting Greek patrons (including actor Telly Savalas) often took part in the exuberant folk dances that ended with a bang of dinner plates being smashed on the floor.

The Grecian Gardens closed in 1979, but Koropoulis didn't leave the restaurant business. He eventually owned or co-owned twelve eateries, including Grecian Nites and Never On Sunday (both on Bolivar Street).

In 1980, the Cleveland Comedy Club moved into the space vacated by the Grecian Gardens. It became a launching pad for future film stars, actors, writers and producers. One of these up-and-comers was Drew Cary, who arrived in 1986 to take a $50 prize on amateur night. He didn't remain an amateur for long—just three months later, he was the club's emcee, earning $100 per week. This was just the beginning of the parade of future stars who started their careers here, including Steve Harvey, Jeff Shaw and Garry Shandling. But after eleven years of entertainment, the comedy stopped when the building was torn down in 1990 for the Gateway sports construction.

Between 1960 and 1983, you could "visit" France if a night in Greece wasn't on your itinerary. Gigi's Montmartre de Cleveland at 2120 East 4th Street offered a menu designed by a French chef who came here from New York's Waldorf-Astoria. Featuring French and American dishes, the restaurant offered coq au vin daily, along with other French delicacies and a French Buffet DeCuisine' every Saturday. Other menu items included chef salad julienne, broiled Mediterranean shrimp, frog legs, lobster Thermidor, Chateaubriand and stuffed boneless chicken breast. A favorite dessert combined crème de cacao and grasshopper crème de menthe with whipped cream. But the supreme after-dinner decadent dessert was the cherries jubilee. A server would come to your table and ignite a pan of cherries combined with Kirschwasser liqueur and then pour the flaming concoction over ice cream. At an outrageous $4.50, this amazing ambrosia was designed to be shared by two.

Irma and George Rassie owned Gigi's, which had an excellent reputation that combined experience, creativity and outstanding customer relations. Their dress code was sometimes enforced by George with unusual zeal. If he happened to notice that an otherwise well-dressed patron had a coat with a ragged inner lining, he would send it out to be repaired while the customer enjoyed lunch. Often these little "clothing side trips" were unnoticed by the guest. Once he didn't like the look of a gentleman's tie, so he clipped it off and gave him enough money to buy something "more attractive."

Actually, George Rassie had a restaurant at the 2120 East 4th location in the 1950s named the George Rassie Restaurant, which he later changed to Roxy's Café. The site had been a saloon or restaurant since the turn of the century, except for five years in the 1930s when it was a retail store. Gigi's became the Apres Vous Café followed by the Star Bar and Grill and then Ferris Steakhouse. Its last occupant was a Harry Buffalo Restaurant. The building is the only one still standing south of Prospect as of 2011.

The Buckeye Building at 4th and Prospect was the site of Anders Cafeteria, which operated for almost forty years. Established in 1923, it could seat four hundred in its second-floor location. The Friday Special of 1942 was beef

Gigi's Montmartre de Cleveland at 2120 East 4th Street. *Courtesy of Alan Dutka.*

4th Street view, 2019. *Photo by author.*

stew (crammed with potatoes, carrots, peas and meat) for twenty cents. In 1949, there was a twenty-eight-cent hamburger steak, and breaded pork chops were thirty-five cents. Flannery's Pub opened in 1997 in the building. With its hardwood floors, mahogany paneling and brass railings, the pub served traditional Irish food and a selection of American dishes, along with a wide selection of beer and Irish whiskeys. The *Irish Voice* chose it as one of America's top forty Irish pubs and restaurants. Dennis Flannery was the owner operator—a third-generation Clevelander.

At 22 and 24 Sheriff Street was the Rathskeller, where Louis Rich would provide dinner music and then go across the street to lead the orchestra at the Euclid Avenue Opera House. It was a favorite for famous actor Joseph Jefferson, who liked its Kartoffel salad and sauerkraut. It opened on October 6, 1900, and was owned by Henry Grebe for the first two decades of the twentieth century. Prohibition crippled the Rathskeller's business, but it survived with menu favorites like blue points, baby lobster and cheesecake. There was a quick-lunch counter that could seat six hundred. During the 1920s, the bar also provided entertainment, including Marjorie Moore and Her Melody Maids—one of the all-girl orchestras that were popular during that era.

Otto Gross tended bar at the Rathskeller, eventually buying it, scaling it down in size and catering to the working man—the "shot and a beer" crowd—instead of the patrons looking for martinis or cocktails.

The Rathskeller moved to Prospect Avenue in 2000 and continued as a workingman's bar. Regulars continued to enjoy beer in frosted glasses until the saloon ended its 110-year run in 2010.

Shop and Stop

Back in the *old* days," shoppers knew that it would be easy as pie to get something to eat during their shopping trips. Most stores had some type of restaurant or lunch counter. The department stores were known for their tea rooms, and the five and dime stores (dime stores) were known for their luncheon areas. They *all* had them.

FIVE AND DIMES

Woolworth's, Grant's, McCrory's—you could always count on them to get good food cheap. During the early days of the civil rights movement, it was a "sit-down" or "sit-in" at a segregated lunch counter at Woolworth's in Greensboro, North Carolina, that made Woolworth lunch counters newsworthy. Sit-downs were held at its counters in cities across the country to protest the store's racial segregation policy.

The Woolworth's on East 4th Street boasted a large lunch counter, as did the W.T. Grant at 330 Euclid when it opened in 1912. Woolworth's Euclid store wrapped around the corner down 4th and had two floors. Woolworth's actually had two stores on Euclid Avenue. Besides the one near Public Square, there was one in Playhouse Square at 1317 Euclid, which closed in 1974.

Grant's opened its first store in 1906. It bucked the trend by calling itself a "25¢ store" to show that it was a few cents above the five and dimes. Like the dime stores, it had lunch counters. It didn't take long for its lunches of hamburgers and hot dogs to become customer favorites. At its peak in the 1960s, it had more than one thousand stores. Like most other stores of this kind, Grant's filed bankruptcy and closed in the mid-'70s. But unlike other stores, it had another "occupation." In 1936, it established a philanthropic foundation "to assist, by some means, in helping people or peoples to live more contentedly and peacefully and well in body and mind through a better knowledge of how to use and enjoy all the good things that the world has to offer them." The foundation was still active in 2020, surviving the stores that went bankrupt in 1976. In Cleveland, its building survives on East 4th as the W.T. Grant Lofts.

Basically, the five and dimes that were ubiquitous from the early 1900s to around 1970 gave way to changes in shopping patterns, as so many department stores opened with a wider variety of items. Over the years, the prices at the dime stores started to climb, and large discount stores like Kmart and Zayre made the dime store obsolete. But they had a good run and served up a lot of lunches for their customers over the years.

MAY COMPANY

Department stores got in on the act too. Most had more than one type of eating area—a more formal restaurant and a lunch counter. May Company was one of the major department stores that opened stores throughout the country. The first May Company in Cleveland (the last major department store to open in downtown Cleveland) was actually the E.R. Hull & Dutton Company, until May Company bought Hull & Dutton in 1899 in a $300,000 merger. The building was on Ontario Street and later expanded onto 158 Euclid Avenue in 1901. It went through many expansions until 1931, when the Cleveland May Company store became the largest department store not just in Cleveland but in the state of Ohio. The Euclid Avenue building completed in 1915 was built by Daniel Burnham, who also designed Cleveland's Group Plan and Mall and the White City for the Chicago World's Fair in 1893. It stands today as a gleaming white terra-cotta structure featuring clean lines and symmetrical details, including Chicago-style tripartite windows facing the Square.

David May, founder of the May Company, grew up in Cincinnati. He and his brother-in-law founded May, Holcomb & Dean (which became May

Company) in Leadville, Colorado, in 1877. The decision to open a store in Cleveland in 1899 was based on the city's spectacular growth during the second half of the nineteenth century. There was an expanding and lucrative retail market that spurred the addition in Cleveland.

The store offered a wide range of goods and services. It even started free home delivery in 1901 and built an indoor playground that accommodated up to 250 children. Other offerings included items not easily available at other stores. It was the sole agent for the Knabe "Mignon" Grand Piano Company. It even had free musical concerts to keep its customers entertained.

Of course, there was also food. On March 10, 1929, a *Plain Dealer* ad announced the opening of its redesigned restaurant, now called the Spanish Room Restaurant and Tea Room, on the fifth floor. Customers could get quality food at reasonable prices. Opening day promised "Music by the Toreador Trio." Described as a "corner in old Seville or the somnolent atmosphere of the Alhambra," everything was new here, including the "carpet in colors like smoldering embers to the rich, warm brown of the arched ceiling." Of course, the china and silver were new as well. The varied menu was overseen by one of Cleveland's most famous chefs, although the ad neglected to mention his name.

Elsa Savenye worked for twenty years at the Mayfair Restaurant, which was decorated in charcoal gray. After her retirement, she reminisced about her days at the department store eateries during the time when "business was downtown, and not suburbia." She recalled that in the '40s "they were the place to go." It was not uncommon for them to serve one thousand people per day.

When she arrived in Cleveland in 1922, Elsa was hoping to be a concert singer but ended up in the restaurant business. Before arriving at May Company in 1942, she supervised the food service at the Hollenden Hotel. She wasn't long at May Company before she took over the management of the employees' cafeteria, where they served 6,800 people every day. Eventually, she became the manager of the Mayfair. She said, "It was hectic—ordering food, planning menus, but I loved it." She claimed that women were fussier about their food than men, and she would know, considering her long career in food service at a number of restaurants. But like anything else, there's always an exception to the rule—one finicky customer actually demanded vinegar on his pecan pie.

In April 1959, you could get a complete chicken lunch or dinner with a choice of soup or juice, half spring chicken with dressing, whipped potatoes, peas, rolls, butter, jellied fruit salad and dessert and beverage for $1.35.

Of course, as May Company expanded into the suburbs, there was a Mayfair Room in each store, so you could shop and eat no matter where you were. But the Mayfair Rooms were not just for eating. Fashion shows, exhibits, lectures and other events often were held in these spaces.

Like other department stores, the May Department Stores Company chain suffered through the years at the end of the twentieth century. During the early years of the 2000s, the store went through several changes—first becoming Kaufmann's then Macy's. Loyal Cleveland May Company customers were not happy. The downtown flagship store closed in January 1993.

STERLING-LINDNER-DAVIS

Of the eight major department stores downtown, Sterling-Lindner was the oldest, starting in 1845 at 187–189 Superior Street as Thomas S. Beckwith Dry Goods Company. George P. Welch and W.R. Havens joined the firm in 1865. Two years later, Frederick A. Sterling came on board, and the store became Beckwith, Sterling and Company. The store grew over the years, and in 1874, it moved from Superior Street to bigger and more modern quarters at 6 Euclid Street. When Beckwith passed away, the store changed its name to Sterling & Company.

Another move was made in 1883 just up the street to 10 Euclid Street, to a building with fancy glass display counters, ornate lighting and thick carpeting. The store specialized in expensive broadloom carpeting, and it started to put in free carpeting for large commercial structures, such as auditoriums, office buildings, hotels and model homes as advertising. This caught the attention of many Euclid Avenue millionaires, who became constant customers. When George W. Kleim invested in the company, it incorporated in 1886 as Sterling & Welch. This change ushered in a more expanded line of products, making it a popular store for Cleveland's elite.

In 1908, construction was begun on a new store at 1225–1239 Euclid Avenue. The $500,000 five-story building designed by J. Milton Dyer featured a steel structure with an exterior of terra cotta. There was a French-styled glass and wrought-iron portico at the entrance, model showrooms, three elevators and a freight elevator and three thousand sprinklers. The building was attached to a warehouse. A state-of-the-art cleaning system and pneumatic messenger service went throughout the entire building. The new store opened in May 1909 and became the city's fourth-largest store.

Expansion of product lines and services continued to the Great Depression and in succeeding decades. Perhaps its most famous addition was its Christmas tree, which first showed up in 1932. It made an annual appearance, and by the 1960s, it was fifty feet high with 1,300 lights, 1,500 ornaments and sixty pounds of icicles. Decorating this gargantuan tree took volunteers some six hundred hours. The Christmas tree remained an annual favorite with Clevelanders.

The tea room of this popular department store opened sometime after 1915, when it was located at 1331 Euclid Avenue; it quickly became popular with its offerings of lunches for sixty-five cents that included choices like club steak dinners with au gratin potatoes or corned beef hash with poached eggs. A new restaurant with "reasonably priced French cuisine"—the Continental—was introduced in 1936.

The store relocated again sometime after 1949 to the corner of Euclid and East 13th in the former Higbee Building. Around this time, the nation's largest operator of department stores, Allied Stores Corporation, made a succession of purchases, including Lindner & Davis and Sterling & Welch. These became the Sterling-Lindner-Davis Company. In 1958, Davis was dropped from the name, and the Lindner Company became Sterling-Lindner Company. Along with other stores affected by suburban flight, it closed on September 21, 1968.

HIGBEE'S

Higbee's department store opened in the Terminal Tower complex in 1931 with twelve stories. There was a tea room on the tenth floor when the store opened that served lunch for one dollar, a salad for sixty-five cents and a tea plate for thirty-five cents. The room offered an à la carte menu of soups and sandwiches and a children's menu. It wasn't until that room became the Silver Grille around 1935 that it became famous. It was described as a tea room extraordinaire with Art Deco design used throughout the whole space. This classic design element extended to the table settings and the elegant menu, which reflected the tastes of the time. The fountain in the center was surrounded by a pond with goldfish and was a favorite of the children visiting there.

The Silver Grille was designed in the "Art Moderne" style by Philip Small of the Small and Rowley Design firm, which also designed the rest of the Terminal Tower internal spaces. Its furniture was designed by William Green and Andrew Probala of Rorimer-Brooks. Guy Cowan, who had previously operated Cowan Pottery in Rocky River and was now working for Syracuse China of Syracuse, New York, designed the china, which complemented the room. Table linens were also Art Deco. The *Plain Dealer* review of the opening noted, "In the tea room Small has used six shades of green in the decoration combined with a silver leaf pattern. Door, window fixtures and furnishings including tables and chairs are in aluminum. For the fountain in the center of the room, Small selected slates of Rojo Alicante marble." It was a triumph of understated elegance.

The Silver Grille was classified as a tea room. Food served there was considered "fussy," dainty and served in smaller portions. Some people claimed that it was "ladies' fare," but others called it WASP cooking. According to early twentieth-century thinking, middle-class women ate foods that were "refined," and they ate less of them and more slowly. It was believed that the color, texture and presentation of a meal was as important as the items that made up the repast. Tea rooms did *not* serve alcohol. Since the Silver Grille opened during Prohibition, that didn't really matter; however, a bar was added in the early 1980s. Chicken à la King was at the top of the food chain in a tea room. Even today it's a favorite on lists of "comfort foods," especially when prepared properly and served on good biscuits. Other tea room favorites included chipped beef on toast, gelatin salad, Welsh rarebit, creamed eggs and tomatoes and, of course, lots of desserts. In 1932, you could get a luncheon special at the Silver Grille that included your main dish, side, dessert and coffee, tea or hot chocolate for sixty cents.

At this time, shopping was serious business, so tea rooms and restaurants in stores were important. Shoppers would often spend the whole day shopping before heading home for supper, so they needed sustenance. Because hotel dining rooms were often considered the only respectable eating places for women, and because most hotels were not close to stores, the department stores needed to fill the void to provide the food. Other Cleveland department stores that had tea rooms were the Minotaur Room at Halle's and the Mayfair Room at May Company.

At the Silver Grille, lunch was served to the accompaniment of the Louis Rich Orchestra, and often there were fashion shows with the latest Parisian styles. Prime rib with Yorkshire pudding was offered for Christmas dinner. There were special menus for children, and their meals were served in tiny ceramic dishes with silverware and a napkin. At Christmas, the children's meals were served in miniature stoves. These wooden containers and metal stoves were replaced by cardboard toy stoves in 1974. Cardboard trucks were added in 1983.

The food and service were held to a high standard—eating at the Silver Grille was an experience. In 1935, the service included finger bowls, after-dessert mints on the Silver Grille china and cheese—just like the best restaurants of the day. In the early days, when people were not concerned about things like cholesterol, the Grille served meat with sauces or gravy, stewed vegetables, salad and the "famous Higbee muffins." Some of the original menus and recipes came from the Schraft's restaurant chain in New York. It had a chain of tea rooms across the country. Chicken was an important part of the menu—so important that one kitchen staff person's entire job consisted of doing nothing but removing meat from the bones.

During its first fifty years, the Grille did not serve a single hamburger, pizza, stir fry or taco. These items did not appear until the 1980s. During this time, the Silver Grille introduced salad bars, buffets and themed luncheons. The other item to finally appear on the menu was alcohol. A Champagne Buffet for the holidays was offered in 1984 for $6.25 for adults ($3.00 for children under ten). The festive feast included chilled fruit, quiche Lorraine, seafood Newburgh, chicken fingers, baked ham, broccoli cheese soufflé, blueberry crepes, muffins, rolls, bread, coffee, tea, milk and, of course, Champagne.

Whenever the Silver Grille stayed open for dinner, it would have a different menu, which included steak and prime rib roast, and the portions were bigger.

Besides serving food, the Silver Grille was a part of the merchandising plan of Higbee's. At Christmas, there was Breakfast with Santa. In later years, there was lunch before or after visiting with Santa, Bruce the Spruce or Mr. Jingeling.

On the opening day of the Silver Grille, there was a full house, and the large crowds continued for the next fifty-eight years until its closing. The Silver Grille's peak period was during the 1930s and '40s. There were sixty to seventy women employed in the kitchen. All the foods were prepared by hand in the kitchen—fruits, vegetables, breads, rolls, cakes, sauces, stocks and soup. The staff started at 7:00 a.m., turning on the steam lines and lighting the gas ovens. They quit at 4:30 p.m. The Grille had seventy-five waitresses during its peak years, but by the 1980s, there were only about thirty-five. Often waitresses were mothers and daughters—it was a family affair. Being a waitress there was considered a desirable job. They went through a rigorous training period, and there were some who started in 1931 and stayed for forty years. The waitress staff got special help from a group called the "party ladies." These women came from a society background. They helped out during special events in the Auditorium lounge and banquet rooms. They would donate their earnings to organizations like garden clubs and charities. The party ladies found this to be a good way to raise money for their favorite organizations and a chance to mingle with the famous people booked for these events, like Amelia Earhart in 1932. Another popular event was the book launch of local TV personality Dorothy Fuldhiem's new work, *I Laughed, I Cried, I Loved*. Nine hundred people showed up at the Silver Grille for the event, which was televised live on WEWS.

During the 1970s and '80s, the Grille could seat five hundred people.

When Higbee's opened the Silver Grille, it was part of a major tradition of department stores—most had tea rooms back then and prided themselves on the service. By the late 1970s, shopping patterns and general downtown activities had changed dramatically. Many retail businesses and theaters closed. Downtown Cleveland was on a downward spiral and in serious trouble. But Higbee's managed to stay open, and so did the Silver Grille, which got a makeover in 1974. The new contemporary look included seven new murals

Higbee's Silver Grille, 1983. *Photo by Richard Karberg from* The Silver Grille, *reprinted by permission of the publisher, Cleveland Landmarks Press.*

and a green, white and yellow color scheme. A third redo was executed in 1983 and kept the original Art Deco feeling with a muted color scheme.

Although the Silver Grille had generally operated at a loss since the beginning, it was such an important part of the Higbee idea of service and promotion that no one really cared as long as the quality of the food and service remained high.

The other restaurant on the tenth floor was the Pronto Room, which shared the Silver Grille's kitchen. Opening in October 1956, it was located in a space previously occupied by a bank of elevators. Set lunches cost ninety cents and were made up of items from the Silver Grille menu. The Pronto Room promised "a delightful lunch in just 20 minutes." It closed in 1983.

Bargain shoppers favored Higbee's basement, where they were able to find a lunch at the Frosty Bar. There were soft drinks, hot dogs and—the *real* favorite—a thick frosted malted drink. This was truly a "bar," as there were no seats there. If shoppers had a little extra time to actually sit down and eat, they could go to Le Bistro on the second floor.

In 1987, Higbee's was sold to Dillard's department store of Arkansas. The Silver Grille closed in 1989 but reopened as an event venue of the Ritz-Carlton Hotel in 2002.

HALLE BROS. DEPARTMENT STORE (EAST SUPERIOR STREET NEAR PUBLIC SQUARE; 89–91 EUCLID AVENUE; 1208, 1218 AND 1228 EUCLID AVENUE)

Joe Halle purchased the old Lyceum Hall in 1870 and renamed it Halle's Hall (East Superior Street near Public Square). On the first floor was the Bavarian Sweet Shop, which sold pastries and candies, with a dining room at the back.

In 1891, Joe's enterprising nephews, Samuel H. and Salmon P. Halle, purchased Paddock & Company at 89–91 Euclid Avenue for $75,000 and opened Cleveland's newest department store. One of their early slogans was "Look at Our Stock before Going Elsewhere."

Starting off as a hat repair shop and furrier, the brothers soon expanded to include shoes, clothing, home furnishings and a mail-order business. Business quickly picked up, and sometime around 1893–98, they moved to more spacious quarters in the Nottingham Building (89 Euclid Avenue);

in 1902, they changed their name to Halle Brothers Company. It quickly became the place to go for the best in fashions and home furnishings.

As their popularity and offerings grew, they soon needed more space. Their next move (in 1908) was to the Pope Building on the south side of Euclid Avenue at East 12th near Huron. It had 140,000 square feet, ten stories and 100 feet of display windows. But even that wasn't enough. In 1911, they unveiled plans for a new building next to the Pope Building (1228 Euclid). They added more space with the Huron-Prospect Building in 1927.

Halle's had several locations downtown, but its most identifiable building was a gleaming terra-cotta building at 1228 Euclid Avenue, which was built in 1910 and had doubled in size in a mere three years. It was designed by architect Henry Bacon, and Owen Coughlin did the interiors. The building became famous as the backdrop for *The Drew Carey Show*.

Halle's backed up to Huron Road and opened an expansion across the street in 1927. Called the Prospect Building, it was originally for home furnishings and men's clothes. But everything was moved back to the Euclid Avenue building in the 1950s, and the Prospect Building served as a parking garage and warehouse. The Euclid Avenue building was expanded in 1949.

On June 6, 1927, *Time* magazine called it one of the best-run department stores in the country. Obviously, Halle's was *the* place to shop in downtown Cleveland for many years. Besides the store itself, it offered special events like

Postcard of the Halle's seventh-floor tea room, 1911. *Courtesy of Alan Dutka.*

JAPANESE TEA ROOM   THE HALLE BROS. CO. CLEVELAND, OHIO.

Postcard of the interior of the Japanese Tea Room, 1918. *Courtesy of Alan Dutka.*

fashion shows, recitals and plays and was a place to dine for the "ladies who lunch." During this time, genteel women considered ordinary restaurants déclassé, and hotel dining rooms were appropriate but expensive. The department store tea rooms solved this problem with their refined food for "upscale retail" clients. The Halle's Tea Room was a favorite spot for women shoppers and socialites. It also supplied the food for the programs that took place on the seventh-floor auditorium. The Halle's Tea Room started a department store tradition in Cleveland.

One of its first stores included a tea room on the seventh floor so that women could have lunch and shop or go to a matinee at one of the many vaudeville theaters by the store. The tea room was a new idea, but it looked like it was already one hundred years old. It had English oak paneling with hand-carved molding. The plaster was antique ivory. There were leather-upholstered side chairs and oak tables. Copper-colored lights bathed the room. Many remarked that it reminded them of the dining room at Halle's Hall. There were two areas reserved for private luncheons, which were advertised as areas for women who could "not find help to prepare and serve a luncheon at home." Fresh flowers, colored place cards and favors were arranged by a hostess, who suggested an appropriate menu, which often included four to five courses. Meals often began with a fruit cup followed by a cream soup or consommé. After that, there would be sweet breads, chicken breast or squab, salad, dessert, coffee, bonbons and nuts.

Opening day at the tea room had 70 "maids" who served 1,500 customers by 3:00 p.m. Halle's did not want any customers getting preferential treatment because of lavish tips, so it not only paid its waitresses a salary above industry standard but also printed a message on its menu: "It is the rule of this establishment that no gratuities be accepted by any employee."

Around 1918, Halle's opened three new dining rooms on the seventh floor: the Italian Renaissance Men's Grille, where smoking was allowed, and the Colonial and Mandarin Tea Rooms, which were for the ladies and where no smoking was allowed. The Tea Room Christmas Tradition was to serve children a hobo luncheon, complete with a kerchief wrapper.

The Colonial was done in Neoclassical style and paneled in English oak with antique ivory plasterwork. The look was completed with oak tables, leather chairs and copper lights.

The tea rooms closed sometime in 1923 because there was too much competition from all the restaurants that had opened in Playhouse Square down the street. Shortly afterward (circa 1930/32), a luncheonette was put in at the downstairs level. It had eighty-eight stools and a limited menu, but it turned a modest profit.

The tea room became the Minotaur Room in 1956 and was designed by Daniel Rassmusson. It featured murals in the style of Matisse and Picasso that told the legend of King Minos. There were brochures at the checkout that told the story of the themes painted on the panels.

Later, the Minotaur Room became the Geranium Room. The flower was a favorite of Blanche Halle, the owner's wife. It was often used in the store's advertising. The Geranium Room and Minotaur Room were both popular spots with shoppers over the years, and there was an informal luncheonette in the basement. In 1961, the Minotaur Room had a special Thursday night family buffet. The cost was $2.00 for the "host," $1.50 for adults and $1.00 for children. The Halle's restaurants got new menus in 1977 that put an emphasis on healthy foods at reasonable prices. In March, it hosted a benefit for the Playhouse Square Foundation called the Grand Tour. Tickets ran between $7.50 and $25.00 and allowed the nine hundred tourists to "travel" on each floor of the downtown store to find food, drink and music from different cities.

In 1960, Halle's opened a sidewalk café along Huron Road. *Cleveland Press* society columnist Winsor French called it "Café Au Soliel." It opened at 10:00 a.m. with coffee and pastries. At noon, Buddy Grebel played piano for the lunch crowd, who dined on a menu of "salads, sandwiches and tall, cool drinks."

Halle's closed in January 1982. The building was added to the National Register of Historic Places on September 8, 1983. The building still stands, and as of 2019, it is an apartment building with a Yours Truly Restaurant on the ground floor.

MEMORIES

Dodi Lettus wrote on August 3, 2018, that she "used to eat at Woolworth's counter a lot, too, with my school friends. I remember asking a waitress for a glass of water and then asking how much it cost. She indignantly told me that this was the United States of America and we don't charge money for water! How times have changed."

Jan Springer e-mailed on July 9, 2018, to say:

> My favorite memories are of the Silver Grill [sic] up in Higbee's. When we would go downtown with my Mom and grandmother to do shopping, we'd always have lunch at the Silver Grill. How elegant it was. And they had a special lunch for kids, they'd bring out a small "buffett" [sic] and you would set your own table from it. I remember everyone being "dressed." Dresses, hats, white gloves. Tinkling of glassware and china, white table cloths. Real cloth napkins. It always felt so special.
>
> Occasionally lunch was at Sterling Linder Davis—way upstairs and each floor of the store had an opening where you could look all the way down to the lobby. At Christmas they had a huge tree all decorated (per Wikipedia one of the largest in the U.S.), and if you had lunch there you ate looking out at the top of the tree. That was cool, but the Silver Grill is the one that pops back into my mind from time to time.
>
> We are so casual nowadays and have lost that "specialness," that elegance in life. Learning which fork went with what course. Sitting up straight, no elbows on the table. Respect for others. Yeah, it was a hassle, yeah things are much more comfortable and easy nowadays, but I do miss that lifestyle from time to time.

J.H. Flora wrote on June 12, 2018:

The Silver Grille was on the top floor, I believe the 10th, of the Higbee Department Store on Public Square. Once, in the early 1980s, I met my wife and two oldest kids there for lunch. I don't remember the menu but do remember the place had a classy Art Deco design and was suitable for preschool children. My son's lunch came in a box that looked like a Higbee delivery truck and my daughter's in a box that looked like a stove.

Years later, after the store had closed and the upper floors were turned into office space, I worked in the Higbee Building for a few years. At this time, I heard that the renovations had not extended to the top floor and the Silver Grille was preserved intact although it was only used occasionally. During this time, I would sometimes see the distinctive, aluminum chairs from the Silver Grille in the public spaces of the building when they were set up for special events.

Note that the Higbee Department Store was featured in the movie "A Christmas Story." The exterior shows up in the Christmas parade scenes. Ralphie sees the Red Ryder BB gun in the window at the corner of Euclid and Ontario. The Santa mountain was set up on the first floor.

Lee Juratovac wrote on October 15, 2019, "The Silver Grille was so special especially for my 2 daughters—the lovely store and great dishes were fascinating for them. My son only ate his lunch without any impression! When I moved several years ago we finally threw the stove away from the 'play kitchen'!! Many lovely memories were shared at that time!"

Peggie Brown sent this e-mail on June 24, 2018:

My mom, sister and I would take the BRT [Brecksville Road Transit] from Independence to Cleveland (read "downtown" because that is what we called the Big City). The bus made only one stop in Cleveland—at the Terminal Tower, which is where you got off and got on to go back home. My mom would do her shopping at the various stores. Occasionally we were treated to a frosty on the lower level of one of the main stores (possibly May Co.). Lunch occasionally at the Silver Grille. However, usually we ate lunch on the lower level of either Kresge's or Woolworth's at their counter (can't remember which one). My sister and I would feel so grown-up sitting at the counter, eating our BLT's, drinking our milk. People waiting for a seat would stand right behind you.

Judy Skillicorn e-mailed on August 10, 2018:

I remember going downtown with my mother to shop. We would take the rapid transit from Bedford to the terminal tower and enter Higbee's in the basement. Then we would shop around looking for potential Christmas presents. My mother was dressed in heels and gloves and usually wore a hat. At lunch, I would beg her to take me to Mills Cafeteria on Euclid Avenue. I thought seeing all the food choices was the most exciting thing possible. Carrying my own tray at 10 or 11 was exciting and grown up feeling.

I remember when our kids were growing up, the day after Thanksgiving was traditional to go to Cleveland and go shopping and see the decorations in the Higbee's windows. We even took three exchange students with us over the years to experience this magical day. Our kids always wanted to go to the Silver Grill [sic] in Higbee's—a very Art Deco place with live fish. They got their meals in cardboard decorated boxes that looked something like stoves. Then they got to go to the Twigbee shop for Christmas shopping "in private" away from prying eyes. Closing Higbee's was the end of a long family tradition of shopping and going for lunch.

On September 19, 2018, Morris Eckhouse remembered downtown with shopping, baseball and eating:

As a kid, in particular, I remember the Silver Grille at Higbee's and the Minotaur Room at Halle's. I found precious little about the Minotaur Room on the Internet, but it does get a mention in the book Cleveland's Department Stores. *I also remember the Harvey House on the lower level of Terminal Tower. I'd take the Rapid Transit from Shaker Heights downtown, get a hamburger at Harvey House, and then walk down to the Stadium to watch the Indians. Around that same time (early 1970s) I recall a Wendy's on the north side of Euclid Avenue close to Public Square. It may have been one of the first....When I was working downtown in the late 1980s and through the 1990s I'd eat at the Wendy's at the corner of Fourth and Euclid where the Corner Alley is now. I also often ate lunch in the food court at Tower City.*

Mary Tieri wrote in 2019 that in the '70s, she and her friends would go to lunch at Woolworth's lunch counter because it "was inexpensive." In 1973, they had a tradition that they "always went to Captain Frank's for dinner every Friday evening. We miss that place [and] wish they would bring it back." When she was working in downtown, Mary recalled going to Pat Joyce's Tavern for lunch. She said that they had "good food there. People were always so kind." She added, "I loved all 3 of these restaurants. Wish we could bring them back....Great memories of all these places. Those were the days in the '70s."

Nina Bentzen wrote in October 2020 that she worked in the Executive Towers of Terminal Tower for CSX and they employed the Silver Grille's "food and ambiance."

Short Vincent

S ome of Cleveland's most famous and notorious restaurants were the nightclubs of Vincent Avenue Northeast. The land once belonged to an early Cleveland settler named John Vincent. This street, which ran a block north of Euclid between East 6th and East 9th and was only one block long, was nicknamed "Short Vincent" in the early 1930s by press agent/ publicity manager Mitchell Dexter Plotkin. It was *the* center of Cleveland nightlife in the early to mid-twentieth century.

The avenue filled up with restaurants and taverns to accommodate all the guests at the nearby Hollenden Hotel. Residents and tourists were attracted to the street because of its wild reputation, with entertaining establishments that included drinks, delicious food and dancing women. It was said that you could find good food, good gossip and good odds on almost anything on Short Vincent. The classier businesses were on the north side of the street, while the strip joints and gambling houses were on the south. The rambunctious and violence-prone street itself was referred to as "Cleveland's Gaza Strip." In 1958, forty bars existed in the area of East 6th to East 12th between Euclid Avenue and Superior Street.

The Jolly Set was a group of reporters who patronized Short Vincent during its heyday in the 1930s and '40s. It was led by *Cleveland Press* columnist Winsor French. They organized a charity bazaar in 1953 called "Fun for Funds." Booths were set up on the closed-off street, which became a dancefloor. Bill Gordon was the emcee for the event, which was covered as a live event by Channel 9/WXEL. Mel Torme wrote a song about the fair that apparently has been lost to the world. Bartender Richard Tuma, from Mickey's Show Bar, took a perch on a flagpole installed in the street. He advertised the fair from his spot in the air but made a quick trip down to earth when a tornado came through, making a shambles of everything. Another fair was put together for 1954—this time the tornado was *not* invited.

On the south side were the burlesque houses (especially the internationally known Roxy Theater) and the Coney Island restaurant, offering hot dogs and a house special of thirty-nine-cent fried eggs, toast and jelly and coffee for the "after-show" crowd. Underworld figures, mob bosses and gamblers came to the street and were even attracted to the "more respectable businesses" on Short Vincent. The mix of the respectable and the unrespectable places seemed to be part of its charm. Writer Alan F. Dutka remarked that the "Theatrical Grill and Kornman's Back Room created a touch of elegance" in this area where many other establishments specialized in B-girls (bar girls) and striptease artists.

The peak of activity on Short Vincent was in the 1930s and '40s. In 1944, there were fifteen drinking establishments on this short street. But most of the fun had ended by the late 1970s. Cleveland nightlife had moved to the Flats, leaving Short Vincent, well, flat.

East 9th at Short Vincent, 1973. *Photo by Frank J. Aleksandrowicz, National Archives and Records Administration, 550139.*

THE SMALLER RESTAURANTS

A. Jacob's Grill Room was at 811 Vincent. It was replaced by the Taystee-Bar-B-Q. Taystee's food was apparently good enough to steal because in the 1950s, two thieves took off with a spit of around five cooked chickens.

The Wishbone Restaurant (830 Short Vincent) had a tea room cafeteria for women from 1926 to 1932. The tea room became an evening restaurant, serving generous helpings of wonderful food and entertainment. The cook was obviously proud of her dumplings, which were served on Monday evenings. The menu actually read, "Ask for another helping of dumplings and gravy."

Freddie's Café went into the spot of the Wishbone Restaurant when it closed. It was owned by Freddie Meyers. Freddie's offered floor shows and food. For whatever reason, it never got the lowly reputation of its neighbors in spite of the entertainment being described as "girl frolics" and "leg exhibitions." The house orchestra, Freddie Carlone's Swing Band, had a lead singer who earned twenty-five dollars per week by the name of Perry Como. He worked there for three years. Como and the band were basically backup for the "novelty acts." The girlie shows shifted to striptease at the end of the '30s, but in 1939, it was Irish singer Peter Higgins who played to a sold-out house—the largest in Freddie's history.

Freddie's had what had to be the robbery with the most unusual getaway car. The restaurant was robbed on April 24, 1940. A masked man stepped from the washroom and held Freddie and two employees at gunpoint. He got $530 from the cash register and $57.10 from the check room before announcing, "I'm desperate—I want that money." He then got away in a cab.

Freddie's Café became Freddie's Paradise Café in 1941. In 1944, Meyers sold it to Charlie Nagle and bought the Hickory Grill at East 9th and Chester. Nagle sold the Paradise Café to Norman Khoury, who changed the name to the Normandie.

The French Quarter (listed as being on Short Vincent and on Euclid Avenue) apparently had one of the city's most industrious employees. Bobby Wade was the emcee/singer for three years. Simultaneously, he was working at the Theatrical Grill. He also somehow managed to hold down a day job at Greyhound at the same time.

Norman Khoury owned Club Carousel (at East 9th), which eventually became the Fireside Inn; George's Bar, which became the Elbow Room; and Club Carnival (814 Vincent). The Club Carnival became the Frolics (owned by Charles J. Polizzi). The Frolics was sold to "Big

Angelo" Lonardo in the 1960s. It advertised "whiskey and women," and it was exactly what it sounds like. People got a little "overly frolicky" at the bar in 1961. One of the showgirls was hit in the head by a shot glass thrown at her by an angry customer, after which she sued the bar for $35,000. All three establishments were connected by a corridor, and they shared a kitchen and the liquor permit. Ironically, Floyd Gable, who was a district enforcement officer for the liquor board, became the manager of Club Carnival in 1955. All of them had closed by the end of 1955 due to various illegal activities. Khoury's son-in-law Emile A. Easa reopened two of Khoury's bars in 1960 and operated another Khoury establishment on Walnut Avenue near Short Vincent. As for George, he left town to become a bartender at Caesar's Palace in Las Vegas.

Danny's Bar at Chester near East 9th was operated by Khoury's other son-in-law, Daniel G. Rahal.

The Frolics was replaced by the Hustler Club in May 1973. This was actually the most respectable club on the site in decades! It served a hot lunch buffet for $2.25; martinis were $2.00 and bottled beer was $1.50. This upscale club allowed unescorted women in for lunch but not for dinner. The PNC bank building replaced it.

One of the only "good" restaurants on the south side of the street was Stouffer's. It opened in 1940 on Euclid Avenue with a back door on Short Vincent. The décor was oak with red linen drapes and murals of the Canadian Rockies. The name was later changed to the Grogshop, and it became part of the Stouffer's restaurant chain. Originally, this door simply read "Stouffer's," but in 1970, the company began opening a chain of Grogshops. Although Stouffer's had a history of strict policies on waitress garb—including banning seamless hose and requiring waitresses to wear lace-up oxfords, girdles and hairnets—the waitresses at the Grogshop were dressed in micro-mini skirts, boots and blouses with plunging necklines. They were also asked to wear their hair long and loose. This was not only a major departure from Stouffer's usual policy but also a departure from most health department rules about hairnets on servers. But it seems likely that no one minded when the waitresses looked like *that*. The Grogshop closed in 1977/78.

Mickey's Lounge Bar (or Mickey's Show Bar) was owned by Morris "Mickey" Miller and Charles "Fuzzy" Lakis, who was a bookie and gambler. It opened in 1947 and became the most infamous clip joint on Short Vincent. In 1959, Ivan W. Smith of the state liquor enforcement described it thusly: "Morally, this is the dirtiest, filthiest place I've ever been in my life." Occasionally, it advertised that it only served "liquid food." The sign in the window in 1965 advertised "continuous entertainment." When it was finally closed in 1965, it was deemed a "common nuisance" by the fire marshal.

The GILSEY HOTEL was at East 9th on the east side across from Short Vincent.

The OAK CAFÉ AND RESTAURANT at 720–724 Vincent Avenue was owned by Joseph Grogan. According to a postcard description, it was "the most beautiful and most popular café in the city." It had an underpass that connected it to the Star Theatre—a burlesque house on Euclid Avenue. Theatergoers used the tunnel to come over for refreshments during intermission. But the notoriety of the tunnel was eclipsed on August 20, 1917, when Leonard Lyons murdered "Roughhouse" John Murphy there after an argument over competition between downtown gambling houses.

The PARISIAN BAR was next to the Vogue Room of the Hollenden in the 1940s.

PICKWICK RESTAURANT had a main entrance on Euclid and a back entrance on Short Vincent from 1956 to 1965.

The TOWN PUMP BAR was a few doors down from the Roxy on East 9th.

PONY'S CAFÉ (730 Vincent Avenue) was operated by Harry "Pony Boy" Weinzimmer, who acted as host. It opened on April 15, 1940, on the Kornman's site next door to EARL WILLIAMS CAFÉ. When Weinzimmer's half-brother, Leonard Cohen, took over the club after Harry's death circa 1942, he changed the name to the 730 LOUNGE. Located next to Mickey's Lounge Bar, the 730 was frequented by mobsters, lawyers and judges. It was one of the two more infamous places of ill repute on the street along with Khoury's Bar (circa 1953). By 1964, it was listed as a "common nuisance" and closed in 1964, but it later reopened. It finally closed in 1974 and became part of the PNC building.

DE PAREE BAR was next door to Jean's Funny House.

KORNMAN'S

Kornman's on Vincent (East 6th and Euclid) was originally opened in 1913 by William Kornman. Isadore Weinberger bought it in 1935, and in 1939, he moved it four doors east to the corner of East 9th and Vincent. Eventually, Isadore's sons, Billy and Jules, took over running the restaurant.

This page and opposite: Sections of a copy of the 1954 mural by Bill Roberts that featured all the Short Vincent notables, presently at Nighttown Restaurant, Cleveland Heights, 2020. *Photo by author.*

It was a steak and chop house that served its dinners on white tablecloths with cloth napkins—the "headquarters for hearty eaters." It was a hangout for sports and show business people until 1967. Around 1951, Kornman's became the first restaurant in the country to provide transportation from the restaurant to baseball and football games. Because it stayed open until 1:00 a.m., it was particularly popular with late-night diners, sports figures and reporters.

In November 1939, Kornman's moved from 728 Vincent Avenue Northeast to 1788 East 9th Street. The new location was the old location of Fischer-Rohr Restaurant, which had moved to Chester Avenue. The new Kornman's had a main dining room, two private dining rooms and a bar. The front opened to East 9th Street, while the rear of the bar opened to a seafood bar at 817 Vincent Avenue. The opening day included music provided by the Louis Rich Orchestra.

New York performers were booked for Kornman's shows, although it was reported that they often sang "off key." But to be fair, they also often employed more qualified people like Muggsy Spanier (prominent jazz cornet player), Jimmy McPartland (a well-known cornetist) and Juanita Hall (Bloody Mary in both the film and Broadway productions of *South Pacific*). Local favorites included pianist/vocalist/disc jockey Ronnie Barrett and Eva Roberts.

Kornman's walls were paneled in the lower half, with painted birch and wainscoting above. It had hard oak tables. Probably one of the most unique features of this restaurant, though, was a seventy-foot mural that hung over the bar. It was painted in 1954 by Bill Roberts and featured all the Short Vincent notables. It was eventually donated to the Western Reserve Historical Society, and a copy of it hangs in Nighttown Restaurant in Cleveland Heights as of 2018.

William "Squeaky" Hilow was the bartender and bookie at Kornman's. One day, Cleveland disc jockey Big Wilson used a walkie-talkie to complain that the service at Pat Joyce's was poor. He pleaded for someone to bring him a drink. Hilow heard the plea, and because he was the kind of bartender who knew his customer's taste, he made a scotch and soda, walked down East 9th and delivered the drink to the still-waiting Wilson at Pat Joyce's.

Kornman's closed in 1967.

THE THEATRICAL GRILL (711 VINCENT AVENUE)

As early as 1885, a music hall occupied the site on Short Vincent that would become the Theatrical. Opening in 1937, the Theatrical Grill became one of Cleveland's best-known and most infamous spots and one of the longest-running jazz joints in the area. In spite of this, it is something of a restaurant riddle. Why was it so popular? Its food and entertainment were good, but Kornman's had a better reputation for good food, Freddie's had more expensive and elaborate stage shows and many other places had bigger stars. Many of the other clubs had a more intimate ambiance. Still, the Theatrical was considered the premier place to see and be seen.

Morris "Mushy" Wexler was one of Cleveland's more infamous mobsters and gamblers. Wexler originally called the place Mickey's Theatrical Grill because he opened it with his brother-in-law, Mickey Miller. Their restaurant was probably the only place in Cleveland where judges, lawyers and felons sat together in one place. Winsor French, *Cleveland Press* columnist, described it as "the only part of Cleveland that literally never goes to bed. It slows down, but it's never quiet for very long."

It hosted top stars like Judy Garland and Dean Martin and was the place to get in on the gambling for sporting events—mainly because of its notorious owner. Not coincidentally, it also was the headquarters of Alex "Shondor" Birns, a notorious Cleveland mobster. In the 1940s, Birns became part owner. Eddie Hallal and Anthony (Nino) Rinicella were the bartenders. They recalled that although Birns was known to the police as a "notorious hoodlum," to the bartenders who served him, he was a "perfect gentleman, a generous tipper and a soft touch." Rincella said that Birns always drank scotch—that is, until the day before he died, when, for some inexplicable reason, he ordered a beer. Birns's wake was held at the Theatrical. There were lots of people in attendance, and some speculated that FBI agents attended too.

When Dean Martin was performing with the Sammy Watkins Orchestra at the Vogue Room in the Hollenden Hotel, he would come over to the Theatrical to join in for impromptu jazz sessions. Many big names in jazz were booked into the Theatrical for runs of six nights a week for several weeks, including Bobby Hackett, Jack Teagarden, Earl "Fatha" Hines, Gene Krupa, Wild Bill Davison, Oscar Peterson, Dorothy Donegan, Dizzy Gillespie, Marian McPartland and her trio, including Joe Morello and Billy Butterfield.

The Theatrical's list of visiting celebs was equally impressive: heavyweight champion Joe Louis and actors Jayne Mansfield, Mamie Van Doren, Don Ameche, Yul Brynner, Victor Borge, Edward G. Robinson, Judy Garland and even Frank Sinatra. In 1954, Rodgers and Hammerstein celebrated the third anniversary of the Broadway opening of their show *The King and I* with a private party there.

Because of the club's notoriety, Wexler asked famed jazz photographer Gene Bixby not to take pictures there because he might take pictures of men whose wives didn't know they were there.

In 1945, the Theatrical was remodeled and expanded, creating an elevated stage inside a curved bar. The Burgundy Room, for private parties and meetings, opened in 1946. The Penthouse and Grill Room were opened in 1950 for group gatherings. At this time, a full-course Thanksgiving dinner served there cost $3.25.

The year 1960 was not a good one for the Theatrical. There was a disastrous fire in September, with fire engines all over Short Vincent, Superior Street and East 9th Street. It took firemen some five hours to get the fire under control. The Theatrical was destroyed. The only thing that managed to escape was a bottle of scotch. Rebuilding started almost immediately. During the construction, Wexler managed to keep most of his

Postcard of the Penthouse at the Theatrical Grill. *Author collection.*

employees on the payroll and his customers supplied by renting a corner bar at the Hollenden. Ground was broken on the new Theatrical on October 19. One year and $1.2 million later, it was reopened with Jonah Jones, jazz trumpeter, on the bandstand. It could serve 750 diners concurrently. The main floor restaurant could seat 220 people. The kidney-shaped bar could accommodate 52 people, while 100 people were in the Caucus Room in the basement. The Commerce Club was on the second floor. During lunch, it was for members only, and in the evenings, it was for private parties; it had a seating capacity of 350.

Favorite foods during the mid-1960s included little-neck steamed clams (eighteen for $2), Chateaubriand for two ($15), broiled lobster ($6.50), Black Angus T-bone ($6), beef stroganoff cooked with vodka ($4.75) and cheesecake, apple pie, lemon pie and double-chocolate sundaes with fudge for dessert.

The 1960s saw jazz artists like Clark Terry, Jimmy Forest and Dizzy Gillespie performing at the restored Theatrical. One particularly busy artist was cornet player Muggsy Spanier, who generally played at Kornman's. One day in August 1963, he played at the Theatrical and at the Cleveland Browns half-time show.

After 1979, pop performers began to invade the jazz world at the Theatrical. It was the only nightclub left on Short Vincent by 1980. During this time, the spot continued to offer jazz with players like Bill Doggett, Harold Betters and Glen Covington, who was a particular favorite. Pianist Randy Moroz played for the lunch and dinner crowds.

But these stars were not the only celebrities at the Theatrical. In 1985, the bartender, Anthony D. "Nino" Rincella, became the first Cleveland inductee into the Bartender Hall of Fame. He was one of the club's original bartenders from the 1940s. It was said that he remembered customers' drinks even if he only served someone once. Regular customers had drinks ready and waiting at the bar shortly before they entered. Rincella was eighty-six years old when he passed away in 1998.

Another fire damaged the Theatrical's interior in 1987, but it reopened a few weeks later. Saturday night specials were offered for $9.95, including chicken Romano, veal parmesan, Boston scrod and frog legs Provençale.

In June 1990, the music stopped—fifty-three years after the club had opened. For a few years afterward, Jim Swingos made an unsuccessful attempt to return the Theatrical to its former glory. A sports bar went in after Swingos left, but it failed as well. The building was still standing in 1999—not as a jazz club but as a "gentlemen's club," complete with brass

Above: The Theatrical marquee before the 1960 fire. *The Cleveland Press Collection, Michael Schwartz Library, Cleveland State University.*

Right: The Theatrical marquee, rebuilt in 1961. *The Cleveland Press Collection, Michael Schwartz Library, Cleveland State University.*

The Theatrical Grill reincarnated as a garage. The marquee shows the ghost of the original sign, 2019. *Photo by author.*

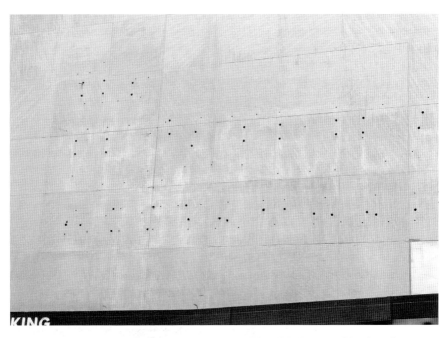

Close-up of the "lost lettering" announcing the Theatrical Grill, 2019. *Photo by author.*

poles. Finally, Wexler's family, Jeff and Buddy Spitz, put the building up for sale, and another local legend faded away to become—what else?—a parking garage.

THE ROXY

Technically, the Roxy wasn't a restaurant. It was a burlesque house. But it's next to impossible to talk about Short Vincent without mentioning this infamous establishment. And to be fair, the building did house two restaurants on the ground floor: the Coney Island and the Little Bar. And after the original Roxy closed, a real restaurant opened in tribute to the theater on the site.

The Family Theater opened in 1903, and in 1907, it became a nickelodeon. In 1908, it was renamed the Orpheum and presented vaudeville. It became a first-run movie theater in 1913 but downgraded to second runs in 1921. In 1931, it reopened as the Roxy, still a movie theater. On October 6, 1933, the movies went out, and the "top bananas" came in—the comics, baggy-pants comedians and strippers.

In the 1930s, the Roxy showcased such acts as Ann Corio, Blaze Starr, Irma The Body, Cindy Parker, Sally Rand and Tempest Storm. In 1933, George Young became the manager. He gave Abbott & Costello and Red Buttons their start at the Roxy. Phil Silvers, Pinky Lee, Robert Alda and Emmett Kelly Sr. also played there; with this kind of line up, the theater soon became nationally known.

The theater chose sex movies over live burlesque in 1938. These were not X-rated but were listed as "sex education." However, this did not last long, and by the 1950s, the strippers had returned.

Remodeled in 1956, the Roxy on Short Vincent continued to be *the* place to go on Friday or Saturday night, although one local paper called it "the city's foremost purveyor of lewd entertainment." It was said that the dancers at the Roxy would sunbathe on the roof and could be seen from the upper floors of the Bond Clothing Store. As the Roxy moved into more illicit programming, you had to be at least eighteen to enter. Of course, that didn't stop the underage boys from trying to get in. One anonymous Clevelander recalled that when he was a teenager, the kids would climb up a step ladder at the building, where the "guards" would take their money and let them in.

By the early 1960s, times were changing, with a significant drop in live shows and a rise in "girly shows" and X-rated movies and nude shows. The Roxy began its downward slide. In 1971, it began only showing adult movies; the next year, the lobby was bombed, which forced a yearlong closing. Some of the neighbors placed signs in their windows pleading, "Do Not Bomb Us." The Cleveland premiere of *Deep Throat* with Linda Lovelace took place there on February 21, 1972. The Roxy limped along until November 6, 1977, when it finally closed for good. A new National City Bank headquarters was built on the site. Stouffer's opened a Roxy Bar & Grille inside the bank building on September 3, 1981, to pay homage to the original, but the reincarnation of the bar had a decidedly different look—live plants, light wood dividers, chrome rails and low reflective ceilings with raised coffers. It had room for 180 patrons. Of course, the biggest difference was that it served food instead of entertainment.

MEMORIES

Tom Roehl remembered that the Stouffer's on Euclid Avenue had its back door on Short Vincent. The men's room window overlooked that alley. At the Roxy, the girls would come out to the catwalk and relax or "sun" themselves, and guys in the restroom could watch them.

Ginny Swift recalled "going to the Theatrical Grill on Short Vincent which was owned by Mushy Wexler, a noted mobster of Cleveland. Mushy was the perfect host as he would circle the room conversing with each table and flicking his Zippo lighter to light your cigarette. It was noted for drawing famous big name entertainers and delicious food. There were always popular athletes, politicians, court personal [*sic*] and notable Clevelanders dining there. You were always sure to see someone famous eating or just 'schmoozing' at the Theatrical Grill."

Morris Eckhouse e-mailed on September 9, 2018: "In the late 1980s and/ or early 1990s my wife Maria and I would go to the Theatrical. I recall Norm N. Nite would come in and play oldies and I think there was a dancefloor. I'd have Caesar Salad. Of course, that was during the final stages of the last version of that restaurant."

Stouffer's Restaurants

Abraham Stouffer and Mahala Stouffer left their creamery business about twenty-eight miles south of Cleveland to open a dairy stand in downtown Cleveland's Arcade Building in 1922. They offered wholesome buttermilk and free crackers. Soon they had a healthy lunch business going. Stepping up their game, they added fresh-brewed coffee and Mrs. Stouffer's homemade deep-dish Dutch apple pies. Stouffer's Restaurants had begun.

Two years and $15,000 later, Abraham and Mahala, along with their son Vernon, opened Stouffer Lunch in a building near the corner of East 9th Street and Euclid Avenue. The restaurant's menu featured four sandwiches priced from twenty to twenty-five cents.

When son Gordon was added to the group in 1929, restaurants in Detroit and Pittsburgh were added to their chain. It was Gordon who realized the importance of coordination in the Stouffer's menus, décor and ambiance. He created standard uniforms for the "Stouffer Girls" (waitresses), along with the slogan, "Everybody is somebody at Stouffer's."

They were such a success that even the Great Depression did not stop them. Their sixth restaurant had opened by 1935, and they made it to New York City in 1937.

In 1940, they were at 725 Euclid. This location featured a weathered oak interior with red drapes and a mural of the Canadian Rockies on the wall. It stayed open until November 1977 and served an estimated 25 million meals before being torn down for the National City Bank's headquarters.

Another Stouffer's opened at 1365 Euclid in 1936 next door to Bonwit Teller's Department store. This restaurant accommodated the wealthy shoppers at Bonwit Teller, and a direct passage was built to connect the store to the restaurant to make eating and shopping more convenient. The first floor featured soda, light lunch and a baked goods counter in addition to the restaurant. Basically, Stouffer's catered to "the needs of the discerning shoppers." It offered "ladylike" cuisine and deft service. In 1938, it expanded the restaurant to nineteen thousand square feet because it was so successful. It could seat six hundred people and was the largest restaurant in Cleveland. This location closed in 1972. Later, the building reopened as a part of the Madhatter's Night Club company as the Last Motion Picture Company—a restaurant featuring "large-screen movies and loud music" (with no connection to Stouffer's).

In the meantime, Stouffer's continued to expand after World War II. Its first opportunity for diversification came when customers at the Shaker Square restaurant went to the manager, Wally Blankinship, and asked him to freeze their favorite items to reheat at home.

Realizing the potential of these frozen foods, Blankenship created the 227 Club, a separate business, to sell the frozen foods. Because it was a restaurant, it specialized in frozen entrées rather than full meals, and because it did not have mass production, its items were of a higher quality and included more meat and vegetables. The business grew so quickly that it started a pilot processing plant in downtown Cleveland in 1954 and officially changed its name to Stouffer Foods Corporation.

John Q's Public Bar & Grille was opened around 1958/59 under the name of the Gaslight Room at 55 Public Square. It became the lynchpin of the Stouffer's Restaurant Chain. The restaurant featured original gaslights from the streets of Bratenahl along with a lounge and a "country kitchen" for regular dining.

The restaurant name was a tip of the hat to the location's history. It was the site of Charles F. Brush's first arc lamp system. Brush was born in Euclid, Ohio, in 1849. One April night, he lit up downtown Cleveland when he built and demonstrated his system of arc lights. At the appointed time, a large crowd gathered around twelve arc lights placed around Cleveland's Public Square. As darkness settled over the city at about 8:05 p.m., Charles Brush raised his arms as a signal. The arcs flared, and the Cleveland crowd was bathed in light. It was the first commercial demonstration of public electric street lighting in the world. The night of April 29, 1879, looked like a day to remember. A replica of one of the lamps hung outside the restaurant.

Around 1979, the Gaslight Room became John Q's Steakhouse, which was shortened to John Q's in 1987. According to its owner, Rick Cassara, in the final twenty-two years it was open, the restaurant reportedly served more than 1 million customers.

John Q's Steakhouse was a classy sports bar in the style of a New York City supper club. It featured local sports memorabilia and a masculine interior of warm lighting, polished brass and hardwood floors. In spite of its decidedly masculine décor, it was considered a romantic spot with a great view of Public Square. Known for its steaks and Caesar salad, other menu favorites included the certified Angus beef porterhouse, black pepper strip steak, bone-in filet mignon, bone-in ribeye steak, lamb, pork chops, a variety of fresh fish, chocolate mousse and apple walnut pie. The landmark eatery closed on June 15, 2013.

The Stouffer's company expanded into hotels in 1960 along with its "Top" restaurants, a series of eateries at the top of skyscrapers in major cities. By 1973, it had six "Top" locations. However, it is unlikely when it opened these high-level restaurants that it thought it would go much higher. The National Aeronautics and Space Administration (NASA) chose Stouffer's to feed Apollo 11, 12 and 14 astronauts when they were in quarantine after their travels. Of course, this fact led to a new announcement: "Everybody who's been to the moon is eating Stouffer's."

Since it couldn't top going to the moon, it did the next best thing: it fed the aquanauts on Tektite II—an underwater research project of NASA in 1970.

Back on dry land, the Top of the Town (1964) in Erieview Plaza in downtown Cleveland was a popular place. It was one of sixteen "Top" restaurants the company opened across the country. The Top of the Town at 100 Erieview Tower was known for its festive atmosphere and its sauerkraut balls. In the 1970s, it had live entertainment by pianist Tommy Clair and musician Gary Lyman. Jack Reynolds of WHK 1420 conducted live broadcasts from the restaurant, as did WJW. The Top of the Town closed in 1995.

Stouffer's was purchased by Nestlé in 1973. In 1975, Stouffer's acquired the Rusty Scupper chain from Borel Restaurant Corp. By that time, the company had about sixteen hotels and sixty restaurants.

Cleveland's Rusty Scupper was located at 1316 Huron Road (corner of East 14th and Euclid Avenue). It opened in 1974 and quickly became the "in place." The site had previously been the Black Angus Beef House, and the redesign cost about $600,000. A wall of concave and convex windows was inserted into the old bricks of the Angus. It had an atrium and skylights in

Interior of the Black Angus. *Courtesy of Alan Dutka.*

The Rusty Scupper featured a massive curved atrium and a skylight feature. *The Cleveland Press Collection, Michael Schwartz Library, Cleveland State University.*

twelve thousand square feet of space, with seating for three hundred. It was perfectly situated near parking and all the theaters in Playhouse Square. The menu was mainly steak and seafood, with prime rib available in two sizes in 1979 for $7.95 or $9.25. The Scupper had a good run and closed in March 1984, to be replaced by Sweetwater Café.

The business continued to grow over the years. What started as a family-owned dairy stand and small restaurant grew into a chain that had seventy-eight units, an award-winning hotel group and an internationally recognized producer of frozen foods that revolutionized the frozen food industry and supplied cafeterias, restaurants, hospitals, schools and commercial/industrial establishments. The company became a legend for quality, made possible by the quality of its employees.

Downtown Cleveland Stouffer's establishments included Stouffer's Lunch (East 9th Street), Roxy Bar & Grill (Short Vincent and Euclid Avenue), Rusty Scupper (East 14th and Euclid Avenue), the French Connection (Terminal Tower), Top of the Town (Erieview Tower) and John Q's (Public Square).

MEMORIES

Employee Tom Roehl remembered in a September 28, 2018 interview that at the Stouffer's by Bonwit Teller, they had ornate glass chandeliers that were dirty, so Tom told a busboy to clean them. Tom got ammonia water and a step ladder and told the busboy to wipe them down. Suddenly there was a crash. The busboy had turned the chandelier instead of moving the ladder and had unwound it, so it came crashing to the floor. Luckily, it was mainly only bent, and they were able to get it back up. It stayed like that until the restaurant closed.

Stouffer's had standards for its cocktails, which included a special large stuffed olive for the martinis. These were very expensive. Tom thought that they should get cheaper olives to save money. Tom went to Brooklyn, New York, to check out the place where they bought the olives. He discovered that the olives came in kegs. So he had a whole keg shipped back to Cleveland. When the olives arrived, the driver slipped, the keg split and the brine came flowing out. To salvage the situation, Tom had to sell the olives to restaurants, so he mixed up a brine to save them and then sold them as soon as possible.

Lynette Filips remembered on October 29, 2018, that around 1970:

I was a home economist working for the Cleveland Electric Illuminating Company (CEI) at 55 Public Square. There I became acquainted with the multitude of restaurants which Stouffer's (founded in Cleveland!) operated, because one of them was right inside the door on the first floor of CEI's building. We girls rarely—or never!—ate there on our own, though, perhaps because it was the place where our supervisor took us for our annual performance review, as well as any other time she had something to say to us about our performance. I couldn't tell you a single food item I ate during those lunches, but I will never forget what she ordered every single time—a bowl of mushroom soup with melba toast!

About the Top of the Town, Lynette wrote that it

was the restaurant "to die for" on East 9th Street. My first experience there was early in 1966; the occasion was Junior Ring Day at Nazareth Academy in Parma Heights. After the ceremony at the school, small groups of girls got together for dinner (and often a movie) afterward at the best place they could afford. In my friends' case, it was taking the bus downtown to eat at Top of the Town (and then flagging down a taxi to get us to the Yorktown Theater in Old Brooklyn in time for a late screening of My Fair Lady).

A couple of decades later I enjoyed revisiting Top of the Town with vouchers I'd won from WQAL's Larry Morrow. In the era before anyone could easily look up the answers on an electronic device, Larry hosted a couple of weekly trivia contests on his morning show. Monday Morning Mind Mania was the one which ran the longest, but winners in both contests received super prizes, including theater tickets and the vouchers to fine dining establishments like Top of the Town and The French Connection.

J.H. Flora sent this Top of the Town memory on June 12, 2018: "This restaurant was in the top floor of Erieview Tower and had a magnificent view of the city and the lake. My favorite memory was an evening in the mid-1980s when we celebrated a wedding anniversary. We had Caesar salad prepared tableside and spent the evening watching airplanes heading toward Cleveland Hopkins Airport. They would come in over the lake, turn over downtown and head straight toward the cluster of lights on the western horizon that was the airport."

Morris Eckhouse recalled on September 19, 2018: "For many years, Top of the Town was a destination to celebrate special events. John Q's on Public Square was another favorite, especially because of its sport memorabilia. We also liked the New York Spaghetti House on East Ninth Street."

Sweetwater Café

1316 Huron Road

n 1984, Gary Lucarelli announced that he planned to reopen the old Black Angus/Rusty Scupper restaurant as the Sweetwater Café in June. Plans included new menu choices like California cuisine with fresh fish, a pasta bar and Angus steaks. Besides feeding the body, Lucarelli planned to feed the soul with entertainment provided by a multitalented wait staff that would perform eight-minute "time capsules" of Playhouse Square history. These "minimusicals," directed by Bill Roudenbush with musical direction by Evie Rosen-Morris, would tell the story of historical happenings at Playhouse Square. Of course, there was also the hope that the additional effort put forth by the staff would be rewarded with bigger tips.

In October, Yul Brynner was the guest of honor for an après-theater party at Sweetwater. *The King and I* was opening at the State Theatre, and the next night would be Brynner's 1,300[th] performance with that touring company. The festivities included a special musical salute to the star, who stipulated that he would listen to anything as long as it wasn't from *The King and I*— understandable after having sung those lyrics so many times.

Although big names were often found at Sweetwater, sometimes it was the talent of an unknown that captured the attention at the café. One such night happened in January 1987 when waiter Tyrone Williams finished his sax solo of "A Child Is Born." After that stunning performance, the diners did something that had never happened before at the Sweetwater: they gave him a standing ovation.

The twenty-two-year-old Williams was in Cleveland for two years as a graduate assistant for Professor Howie Smith at Cleveland State University. Besides waiting on tables, practicing and studying, Williams kept busy appearing with jazz groups at such places as Peabody's, Club Isabella, Reasons Why and Maxwells. Unfortunately, some of his relatives didn't approve of his jazz performances. They preferred that he remain true to his gospel roots. The musician pointed out, however, that both gospel and jazz derive from African roots. He explained, "In slave days, the way music was treated in the spirituals and hymns was an outreach linkage for the blues, then it was jazz."

Starting as a computer science major at the College of Wooster, he later switched to music. After graduation, he moved to Cleveland and started as a busboy at Sweetwater Café while he trained as a waiter. In between the food, he served up crowd favorites to feed the spirit like "Ain't Misbehavin'" and "Don't Get Around Much Anymore."

The downstairs of the café originally housed Luke's Bar and Grill, but in 1987, $150,000 was put into remodeling the space into Hemingway's Key West Grill, where the décor was bright with airy pastel colors and the lunch menu included hamburgers, salads and fresh Florida seafood with Caribbean specialties. Key West Conch Chowder went for $1.95, coconut shrimp for $5.50 and stir-fried duck $5.25. What would a Key West Hemingway restaurant be without an "Old Man and the Sea" selection of charbroiled fish? Fresh shark, grouper, swordfish, dolphin, red snapper, pompano and halibut completed the menu. Plans for the future included adding special tropical drinks to complement the tropical atmosphere.

There were three sections in Hemingway's. There was a library portion with books, and a bar area played off the writer's fascination with hunting. Large animal heads and fish decorated the walls, as did photographs of Papa Hemingway. In the veranda area, there were colorful pink flamingos with attractive plants.

In 1988, Giant Portions, a Cleveland improv troupe, began offering entertainment in the Grill. But by August, Sweetwater's food and entertainment had come under the shadow of a wrecking ball. Lucarelli made plans to move the restaurant to his Café Sausalito at the Galleria at Erieview after the September 2 closing. The merged restaurants were called Sweetwater Café–Sausalito and carried over some of the café's favorites, like the fresh seafood entrées and Cobb salad.

Sweetwater was a formidable force in the resurgence of Playhouse Square and the theaters in the district. Lucarelli not only provided theatrical entertainment in his restaurant, but he also packaged the theater productions with dinners, promoting both the restaurant and the shows together. The restaurant held so many memories that prior to its closing, customers wanted to take home the bar stools where they had sat for their after-work drinks. Most of the items in the restaurant went up for sale, except for photos of Michael J. Fox, Yul Brynner and Alan Alda. Although theatergoers were going to miss their special "show place," Lucarelli planned on offering free bus and parking service to Playhouse Square from the new digs at the Galleria.

MEMORIES

On September 12, 2018, Karen Jones recalled that the menus of the Rusty Scupper were on wooden oars; she went there before going to see the plays at the Hanna Theatre.

Terminal Tower Site

The area on the southwest side of Cleveland's Public Square is arguably the birthplace of all things Cleveland. For as long as there have been Clevelanders, there have been homes, businesses, restaurants, hotels and more—everything on this plot of land. You'd need a scorecard just to follow the restaurant and hotel lineup, and that doesn't even count the stores, businesses and other residents of the area. First, let's look at the early hotels and restaurants on this spot.

Mowry's (Mowery/Mowrey) Tavern was basically the first-known restaurant in town. It was owned and operated by Phinney (Plinney) Mowry and opened in May 1815. He bought Lot no. 82 at the southwest corner of Superior Street from Samuel Huntington for $100 in 1812. Then he built a small log structure that became the first in a continuous line of taverns and hotels on the site. Mowry's Tavern had the distinction of being the location of the city's first theater performances, which were held in the dining room; apparently, it became Cleveland's first dinner theater. Mowrey sold it for $4,500 to Dr. Donald McIntosh in 1820. McIntosh changed the name to the Cleveland Hotel or Cleveland House and turned it into a two-story building with a belfry. Around 1824, James S. Clark bought it, tore it down and built the Cleveland House Tavern and Hotel. It changed hands again and in 1837 became the City Hotel; by 1842, it was in the possession of a James W. Cook, who called it the Cleveland Temperance House (of course, no liquor was sold there). After the tavern burned in 1840 or 1845, it was rebuilt as a four-story brick hotel by David Dunham in 1848 and called the Dunham

Terminal Tower site, 1905. *The Cleveland Press Collection, Michael Schwartz Library, Cleveland State University.*

House. William Smith then bought the hotel 1852, enlarged it and named it the Forest City House. It was *the* place for Cleveland's social and commercial happenings with the city's movers and shakers until it closed in 1915.

The Cleveland Hotel, which replaced the Forest City House, had a coffee shop and a dining room. Breakfast was $0.25, lunch was $0.50 and dinner was $0.75. There was also a dining room, which offered dinners at $1.15 or $1.25.

Scorecard thus far: seven names in one hundred years. But wait—there's more!

HOTEL CLEVELAND/SHERATON CLEVELAND/STOUFFER'S INN ON THE SQUARE/STOUFFER'S TOWER CITY PLAZA/STOUFFER RENAISSANCE CLEVELAND HOTEL/RENAISSANCE CLEVELAND

The Hotel Cleveland opened on December 16, 1918. It was designed by Graham, Burnham & Company, had fourteen stories and one thousand rooms and cost $4.5 million. This extravagant hostelry had a grand lobby (with twelve marble columns that were eighteen feet tall) and lines of gold leaf and arches across a speckled-blue ceiling. The lobby was raised from the ground floor and accessed from entrances on the Public Square side and the Superior Street side by wide marble stairs. The lobby itself included a lounge, a reading room, a cigar stand, a telephone room, a men's café, a kitchen and the main dining room. The lobby was described in the *Hotel Monthly* of February 1919 as, "a wonderful room both architecturally and in scheme of decoration and furnishment....The floor is of pink Tennessee marble, the walls of Tennessee marble to a height of eighteen feet" with pillars going up to cathedral arches. The color scheme was ivory, gold and blue, with walnut woodwork. The ground level itself provided public spaces—a main grill room, a quick-service lunch, a buffet, a barbershop, women's hair dressing, a manicure parlor and billiard room.

The Hotel Cleveland's dining rooms could serve 1,245 people and included a main dining room, a grill, a lunch room, banquet halls and five private dining rooms. The main restaurant was in the lobby and could seat 325. Its color scheme was French gray, blue and gold; chairs were made of walnut with blue upholstered backs and seats. Crystal chandeliers hung from the ceiling. The china was decorated with a figured band in blue and gold and a crest; glassware was bell-shaped; the silverware was Gorham; and the tables were covered with Irish linen.

On the ground floor was the grill room, which seated 275; 127 diners could be accommodated in the lunch room at four horseshoe counters. Food was prepared in a quick-serve kitchen. The space was decorated with white tile walls with framed green panels and white counters. It offered "prompt service at minimum prices."

There was also the intimate Bronze Room and the private Rose Room for the dining pleasure of the guests. Opening-day dinner cost five dollars, and 1,900 guests were served in three hours! Author Michael DeAloia wrote, "It was a sumptuous place that spoke to its guests and offered the allure of something special and different."

The Bronze Room, which had a club-like atmosphere, also functioned as a dance room with bronze-tiled walls and a walnut bar. Entertainment was provided by big bands that played there every night of the week, and WHK broadcast the Murray Arnold Orchestra from there. It was *the* place for mingling with high-society figures and newsmakers.

For years, the Hotel Cleveland was the city's most prominent social and business address, playing host to countless local leaders and world celebrities, including Charles Lindbergh, President Harry Truman and First Lady

Postcard of the Hotel Cleveland. *Author collection.*

Eleanor Roosevelt. But as far as Clevelanders go, perhaps the most important regular at the hotel was Eliot Ness, the city's celebrated safety director.

Eliot and his wife, Evaline, were frequent patrons at the Bronze Room. They mingled with the high society and newsmakers. Eliot felt safe there— he unwound and let his guard down (sort of). He was known to avoid nightclubs because of their mob connections. However, even at his "comfort spot" in the Hotel Cleveland, he always sat with his back to the wall facing the door. In spite of his caution, though, Ness never wore a gun. He did wear an empty shoulder holster, though, apparently "to give the criminals the impression that he might be armed."

The hotel changed names, interior styles and decorations like a teenage girl changes clothes. In 1958, the Sheraton hotel chain acquired it and changed the name to the Sheraton-Cleveland. Renovations started and included a new $5.2 million ballroom. But with the downtown area changing from retail to offices/services, the hotel began to fail in the 1960s.

The Stouffer Corporation bought the hotel in 1978, and it reopened as Stouffer's Inn on the Square. It was modernized and redecorated during this time and again in 1986. The company's restaurants included the French Connection (Continental menu, prix fixe), the Café on the Square (with seating for 150 located in the lobby and serving Continental breakfast, light lunches, pastry, coffee or tea), Mowrey's (an informal lobby lounge that replaced the Bunch of Grapes and had a capacity of 100) and the Brasserie (an all-day dining facility taking over the old Town Room and seating 125).

The French Connection opened in April 1978 in the former Falstaff Room. It could seat 125 customers, who would dine on "sophisticated but not stuffy" French cuisine. Manager Anton J. Pringer predicted that women would love it and that it would become "the place to come and celebrate a special occasion."

By 1989, the restaurant had become a Cleveland classic and was serving an assortment of dishes. Its smoked salmon appetizer and Pommes Anna ($8.50) were called "outstanding" by reporter Holly Collins, who went on to describe the potato dish: "Here was creative genius—a pinwheel of excellent quality smoked salmon slices, topped with a delicately browned miniature pommes anna, slightly smaller in diameter than the salmon pinwheel. The whole gave the effect of a two-toned chrysanthemum. A sprinkling of caviar, light horseradish cream sauce and dill sprigs, were compatible companions to the imaginative duo." On the same menu was a lunch appetizer of warm squab salad with truffled vinaigrettes ($8.95) and entrées of Dover sole with capers ($22.00) and roasted prime veal chop with reduction sauce with a touch of lime ($22.95). Dessert was not lacking at $5.50 each, with choices of black currant tart, a chocolate Armagnac torte and apple tarte Tatin. It remained at the top of the Cleveland restaurant list until it was replaced in 1992.

As plans were being made in 1989 to convert the Terminal concourse area into a shopping mall, the name was changed to Stouffer-Tower City Plaza. When Renaissance International bought it in 1993, it became Stouffer Renaissance Cleveland Hotel—using all of its former names! Three years later, the Stouffer affiliation ceased, and the name was shortened to the Renaissance Cleveland. Score card thus far: twenty names.

When the hotel was owned by the Sheraton, one of its more popular places was the 1961 Kon-Tiki Room (the reincarnation of the Hotel Cleveland's Bronze Room). The Kon-Tiki was the third in the Steven Crane chain that was built in partnership with Sheraton hotels. Walking into the Kon-Tiki was like walking into a little Polynesian paradise—a far cry from the normal Cleveland sights and weather, particularly in the winter. It could seat 230 diners in a room decorated with pools, waterfalls, a Maori long hut, a luau garden and a bridge. The restaurant closed in 1976, leaving Clevelanders to brave the weather once again.

The next iteration of high-quality restaurants in the hotel saw the French Connection turn into Sans Souci. This dining establishment, part of the

A bit of Polynesia in Cleveland at the Kon-Tiki in the Sheraton Cleveland Hotel. *The Cleveland Press Collection, Michael Schwartz Library, Cleveland State University.*

Doorway to San Souci in the Renaissance Cleveland, Terminal Tower, 2019. *Photo by author.*

Stouffer Tower City days, was considered a premier restaurant and "carefree culinary experience"—in fact, the name itself meant "without worry." The restaurant opened in 1992 under Master Chef Claude Rodier. The décor consisted of polished hardwood floors, rich tapestries and lush murals of the Mediterranean seacoast. There were two "prime" tables that were in front of a grand window overlooking Public Square, providing a magnificent view of the city—especially on a moonlit night or during the holidays, when the festive lights would make the Square come alive. In spite of these feasts for the eyes, it was the food that took center stage at Sans Souci. On the restaurant's first anniversary, there was a special "Lobster Menu" that featured Lobster Fricassee with Champagne, leeks and artichokes; Champagne Batter–Fried Lobster with lavender honey mustard; and Lobster Thermidor with linguine primavera (of course, you could order it just poached or grilled if your tastes leaned in that direction). The Lobster Bisque (which was on both the regular menu and the special one) was thick and creamy and served with chive-cheese straws. Other standard items included a house salad with tart balsamic vinaigrette and a Sans Souci Caesar Salad with a whole heart of Romaine awash in a pool of dressing and a hint of anchovy. Desserts included crème brûlée, fresh pear tart and flourless chocolate torte. Thirty some years later, the restaurant is still serving diners. Score card thus far: twenty-two restaurant names.

But we can't talk about all these hotel restaurants, sitting on this prime piece of real estate, without talking about what's attached to the hotel—whatever its name is now.

TERMINAL TOWER

The Terminal Tower is the "city in the city" that has become *the* symbol of Cleveland.

In 1920, two middle-aged brothers decided that it was time to fulfill their boyhood dream of building something *really big*. Oris Paxton and Mantis James Van Sweringen had their eyes on thirty-five acres of land in one of the most dilapidated sections of the city of Cleveland. It was a section of town populated with bohemian musicians, pawn shops, vagrants, seedy vaudeville theaters and beer halls. In this space, the brothers boasted that they were going to tear down more than one thousand buildings, move 3 million cubic yards of material and build the largest building in the world outside New

Postcard of the Terminal Tower. *Author collection.*

York City. The building would have restaurants to feed ten thousand people, a train station, a hotel, an office building and a department store.

Enormous steam shovels were brought in, and they took one whole bank of the Cuyahoga, buildings and all, and dumped it on the other side of the river. Eighty-seven shafts to anchor the tower were dug by hand into the bedrock 155 feet deep. An army of 4,500 men worked twenty-four hours a day all year round, putting the steel skeleton of the building into place, piece by piece. It was dangerous, backbreaking work, and nearly two to five workers died each day—some fell to their deaths, and others were entombed in the cement. But still the brothers pushed on.

For seven long years, the brothers refused to give up. They watched patiently as the tower climbed higher and higher. And finally, on a hot summer day in 1927, the brothers' dream became a reality. There, in the shimmering August heat, stood the second-tallest office structure in the world: a majestic gray granite building with the wedding cake top. Since it was to be the destination for trains from all parts of the country, they called it the Terminal Tower.

The enormous edifice opened on June 28, 1930, with a luncheon for 2,500 guests. It covered 3.5 acres and included the fifty-two-story tower, the Hotel Cleveland, the eighteen-story Medical Arts Building (Republic Building), Builders Exchange (Guildhall) and the Midland Building. Higbee's was still under construction, and the post office was in the planning stages. The cost of the passenger terminal, electrification and approach lines, passenger and freight facilities, engine terminals, rapid-transit lines and the buildings totaled $179 million. At the time of its opening, the 708-foot Terminal Tower was the tallest building in the world outside New York City. The center included restaurants, banks and retail space.

The Harvey Company was responsible for all 175,000 feet of retail space, along with all the restaurants, including the English Oak Room, a tea room and a soda fountain. Fred Harvey (of the "Harvey Girls" fame) was the leader of the Harvey Hotel system that was in use in most of the railroads providing passenger service in the United States. His move into the Cleveland market was considered his boldest to date—it was his first major location east of Chicago and the first with no ties to the Santa Fe railroad system with which he made his reputation.

The English Oak Room was a favorite of the Van Sweringens, mainly because of the English oak used to decorate the restaurant, their private residence and offices in the Terminal Tower. This oak came from Sherwood Forest in England (as in the place where Robin Hood stole from the rich

A figurine of a Harvey Girl. *Courtesy of Virginia A. Going.*

and gave to the poor). Interestingly, the English Oak Room is actually *under* the street, so there are heavy columns in the dining area. It had Belgian marble floors, giving it a truly European look. The walls were oak with inlays of ebony maple and rosewood. It had high-backed leather chairs, and the high-ceiling room brought to mind great baronial halls of an older age. But this was no small English pub— it could seat seven thousand customers, who were greeted by a maître d' and hatcheck girl who remembered every patron's name.

Probably the most exceptional maître d' manager in town was Cecil G. Smith, who presided over the English Oak Room for nearly forty years. Smith began working for Fred Harvey when the English Oak Room opened in 1930, starting as the relief manager of the employees' cafeteria (which became the Acorn Room). He moved up the ladder to the head spot over the next few years, and there he stayed. He was known for his tableside preparations, which were described as the kind that distinguished the good meals from the great ones. It was said that most of Cleveland's top judges and executives knew him, and he had an entourage of loyal waitresses who had worked for him for more than twenty years despite the normally high turnover in restaurant employees. His customers loved him. He was known to provide ottomans for shorter patrons to rest their feet on. Many of his customers tipped him in cigars. Until his heart attack around 1970, he was known to smoke fifteen a day. Those types of tips stopped after that. When he had a laryngectomy around 1947, some of his regular customers took up a collection and paid for the operation and the therapy. With his new voice, he became a member of the Lost Chord Club and helped other patients with the same problem. Smith retired in September 1972 and passed away in May 1973 at the age of seventy-nine.

The 1968 menu of the English Oak Room included appetizers of Cantonese Taste Teasers for two ($4.30) with spareribs, coconut dipped shrimp and rumaki (chicken liver, water chestnut and spring onion wrapped in bacon and served on a bamboo spear), which were served over a hibachi.

The most popular entrée was Steak Diane, flambéed tableside for $5.95 in 1968. Other dinner choices included a combination plate of three baby lobster tails and a petite filet mignon, Cordon Bleu, French pancakes stuffed with King Crab or chicken and Viennese Rostbraten. Dessert specialties were strawberries served alone or with shortcake or on cheesecake. Baked Alaska and cherries jubilee were also available.

At one time, cracks in the street and poor drainage allowed water to come into the restaurant. The wooden paneling and ceiling were almost ruined, and the room was almost lost. However, repairs were made, and the room had become a private dining room as of 2017.

By the 1950s, competition from autos and airplanes was killing off passenger train service. The Terminal Tower was basically, well, terminal. The last passenger train left in 1977. Cleveland's rapid transit trains continued to come into the station, but it was no longer the "landing" place for people coming into town. Like other parts of downtown, it became a shell of its former self. It went through a makeover in the '80s when it was turned into Tower City Center—a downtown shopping mall attached to the hotel and Higbee's. In recent years, Higbee's closed and is now home to Jack Casino. The hotel still stands. Stores and restaurants come and go in the terminal concourse, and it seems that you still need a scorecard to keep track of everything on that site.

MEMORIES

Kon-Tiki

Nancy in Lakewood provided this memory on May 4, 2018:

Well, Jim and I had graduated from college, but because of other endeavors, we hadn't had a chance to get together for about 4 years. I was coming to Cleveland leaving Indianapolis, and coming to Cleveland just for a gathering for my group. And he called me and said, "I'd like to see you." So we went to the…Kon-Tiki Room…after 4 years of not having seen each other. Um, I think we both—over some type of a shrimp cocktail—fell in love that night and six months later we were engaged. Went back several times afterwards because I moved to Cleveland because he was here. And, um, that, that has a very special spot and I'm so glad that the hotel is still there and that they've done such good things.

Janet Revelt sent this story on October 17, 2019: "The Kon-Tiki was an oasis for Clevelanders, especially during our gray winter months. For us, it was a perfect wedding anniversary celebration, considering the date was December 28th. Just stepping through the door, warm South Sea breezes lifted spirits; or possibly it was their famous Mai Tai, meaning 'The Best' in Tahitian—a blend of lime and honey with aged Jamaican rum, enhanced by a touch of ginger."

Lynette Filips remembered this story on October 29, 2018:

> *Cleveland of yesteryear had numerous hotels, but in my 1960s mind, the grandest one was the Sheraton Cleveland in the Terminal Tower complex on Public Square. I know that the Sheraton had numerous dining options, ranging from the Grand Ballroom on an upper level to a British-themed eatery and bar (the name of which I have forgotten) and the Kon-Tiki Restaurant on the lower level. The Kon-Tiki lunch buffet is what we high school girls could afford ($1.99 in those days, if I'm remembering correctly) when we were in the mood for a downtown outing. While I don't remember what any of the main dish offerings on the buffet line were, other than that they were South Seas inspired, I do remember that the dessert was a yummy bread pudding. And the South Seas inspired décor set the mood as soon as one approached the entrance. Two of my best friends and I treated our mothers (and ourselves!) to lunch there in 1967, right before we all left for college/nursing school.*

Harvey Girls

Marlene Spanner Goodman, in an interview on March 21, 2019, described how she was one of the Harvey Girls at the Terminal Tower and only one of two Jewish employees on a team of 350 workers. She got the job through the Jewish Vocational Center, and she loved working for the personnel manager. She remembered that the general manager's wife would take her home for lunch, which was made by their personal cook—something that impressed Marlene immensely. In her day, pregnant women were not allowed to work. When she told her boss that she was pregnant, he asked her to stay until she was "showing" so she was able to collect her paycheck a little longer.

J.H. Flora recalled on June 12, 2018, "There were several Fred Harvey restaurants in the Union Terminal area under the Terminal Tower. The Choo-Choo Lounge was a bar and restaurant with a façade that looked like train cars. There was also a Fred Harvey snack bar. Note that the Fred Harvey chain was featured in the Judy Garland movie *The Harvey Girls*."

The English Oak Room

Marty Perry e-mailed on May 1, 2020, to say:

My husband and I enjoyed going to Cleveland for dinner and had been to a number of the restaurants. Although we had been to the English Oak Room only a few times, we remembered it as being a lovely and elegant place to dine. As the Christmas holidays approached in 1970, we decided to take our daughters who were then 9 and 12 to have dinner at the English Oak Room. We thought it would be fun for them to experience fine dining in a formal and "old world" atmosphere.

Dressed in our best, we arrived at the restaurant. Interestingly, we had the same waitress who had waited on my husband and me once before. She had probably been there forever. The girls were impressed with the dark wood paneling and the formality of the surrounding décor. In talking with my girls recently, they could not remember what they had ordered for dinner, but they did remember dessert. They had ordered a Baked Alaska. They knew it was a very fancy and special dessert, and they had never had it. Well, it came. Their first bites were a big disappointment. They did not like the brandy taste from the flaming at all. My older daughter commented that it was just cake and ice cream with meringue on top. Big deal!

All in all, the dinner was a success, and it was a delightful evening. The girls loved going to a beautiful and elegant restaurant, and even after 50 years they still remembered the occasion.

Winton-Carter Hotel

1012 Prospect Avenue East

Originally, this grand hotel was going to be called Hotel Free after developer J.L. Free; however, the name didn't stick, and it became Hotel Winton in honor of Cleveland automotive magnate Alexander Winton. Doorknobs even had a *W* on them, and some survived into the 1960s. In 1953, when a vice presidential suite was added, it was the first one in the world.

The luxurious Hotel Winton, designed by Nelson Max Dunning of Chicago, was built in 1916. It opened on December 20, 1917, just in time for the Christmas season, ready to party. There was a ballroom and banquet room done in Old English design, with paneled walls and vaulted ceiling and specially designed furniture. The hotel had twelve stories—the first two floors were stone, and the upper stories were made of Blackstone brick and white terra cotta. The six hundred rooms included two hundred that cost $1.50 per day, with the remaining running $2.00 to $5.00 per day. It was a true luxury hotel, since guests could enjoy "washed air year round, and iced in the summer to insure [*sic*] proper ventilation and cooling in all of the dining rooms."

The ground floor had four shops along the Prospect side of the building. The lobby included offices, a grill, a bar and a coffee shop. White marble steps led from the lobby to the mezzanine, where there was a banquet room and a small convention hall that could seat one thousand people. The mezzanine also had six private dining rooms, six lavish suites (including the presidential suite) and offices for the general manager and controller.

There was a large balcony with a view of the lobby and another eight private dining rooms. Above the mezzanine, there were nine floors. Each floor had sixty-one rooms, and all had a private bath and clothes closet—unusual features for that time.

The ninety-eight-by-one-hundred-foot kitchen was in the basement and set up for "all possible future demands of the hotel's business." It included "every conceivable modern device that makes for labor saving, or better serving." Many claimed that the hotel had actually been built around the kitchen. The ranges were constructed with special fuel and burner arrangements and made of extra-heavy steel. Fireboxes were furnished for the gas burners, but coal was also able to be burned. A long service table was in front of the ranges to keep the soups, sauces, vegetables and roasts warm. Warming closets, hot plates, bain-marie heaters and ice coolers were also available.

The Winton was famous for its Rainbow Room—a sunken restaurant four marble steps down from the lobby. Its entrance was from a terrace surrounding the stage and main dining room. Author Michael DeAloia called it a "subterranean mecca of grand entertainment and world-class cuisine." Blue and ivory covered the walls, and silk lanterns lit the room, which could seat nine hundred people. It opened on December 16, 1932, and was an immediate hit as a center for Cleveland nightlife. Besides being known for its world-class food and entertainment, it was the location of some of the first live radio national broadcasts (*Live from the Rainbow Room*). In 1919, the Rainbow Room served dinner and an ice show along with vocal entertainment.

Probably the Winton's biggest claim to fame is that Chef Boiardi ran the Rainbow Room early in his career.

The hotel was renamed the Carter Hotel in 1931/32 after a $700,000 remodeling by Metropolitan Life Insurance Company. At its reopening, a young Rudy Vallée provided the musical entertainment.

Sometime between 1942 and 1958, it was sold to the Albert Pick Company and became the Pick-Carter (with a nod to Lorenzo Carter, Cleveland's first permanent resident and innkeeper). This new iteration did not lack for eating establishments. There was the Lorenzo Carter room on the mezzanine and the Crystal Hall. The Frontier Room opened on September 28, 1956. It was described as "a high-priced saloon with atmosphere of pioneer days" by the *Plain Dealer*. The restaurant was a brick and paneled room with guns on the wall. Branding irons from Texas graced the bar, and other decorations included railroad spikes for coat hooks, paintings of western scenes, Indian

Postcard of the famous Rainbow Room of the Hotel Winton. *Courtesy of Alan Dutka.*

Postcard of the Carter Hotel. *Author collection.*

blankets, feathers and photos of famous outlaws. There were all kinds of antique firearms and knives along with a bullwhip, oxen yokes, steer horns and a coonskin cap. Staff wore western-style clothing.

Managing director Allan J. Lowe hosted an opening-day preview for invited guests. Lowe appointed himself sheriff and wore a western costume that included a matching pair of Colt .45 revolvers with pearl handles and silver barrels. He explained that his guns were "to keep order" as he asked his guests to check their "shootin' irons" at the door. Other rules included requiring "fighting females" to "pick up their mess [hair, torn garments, garters and so on] before leaving the room" and telling the tobacco chewers, "We aim to keep this place clean. Your aim will help."

Grub for the night included hunks of buffalo meat from Chicago. Western music was supplied by Bob Lorence on the accordion, with vocals by Musicarnival's Bill Boehm and a chorus of "tenderfeet" who hummed the second verse to "Home on the Range."

To get service in the Frontier Room, guests had to hit a "genuine spur against a genuine horseshoe," although "genuine" was apparently defined loosely as the "genuine greenery" was plastic. Dining tables were wooden squares with wooden chairs that had red vinyl-leather backs. A large free-standing fireplace was in the center of the room.

In 1968, Andrew T. Ginnan was in charge of the hotel and planning on a $1 million remodeling program to start in 1969. Plans involved a new façade with recessed arches, a new marquee and upgraded corridors and rooms (including putting color TVs in every room). Banquet facilities could handle three thousand people and had been remodeled in early 1968. This hotel was one of the few hotels in the country where food sales surpassed room revenues. Plans were made to restore it to its once grand hotel status, but a major fire erupted on April 14, 1971. It took 135 firefighters and about twenty-five trucks to put out the blaze, which injured 8 people and took the lives of 7 guests, including two cast members of the musical *Hair*, which was playing at the nearby Hanna Theatre. Arson was suspected, as the fire apparently started in the kitchen area of the Crystal Ballroom or Embassy Room and went up the main stairway to all ten floors. The restoration plans also went up in flames.

The hotel closed after the fire. The building is now a senior apartment house known as Winton Manor.

Bibliography

Albrecht, Brian, and James Banks. *Cleveland in World War II*. Charleston, SC: The History Press, 2015.

Alleman, Lisa, and F.X. O'Grady. "Hotel Cleveland." *Cleveland Historical*, May 21, 2012. https://clevelandhistorical.org/items/show/465.

Anders postcard, back description. Cleveland Memory Project. http://images.ulib.csuohio.edu/cdm/ref/collection/postcards/id/424.

Baranick, Alana. "Larry M. Mako, Co-Owner of Hickerson's at the Hanna." *Plain Dealer*, July 10, 2000.

Barmann, George J. "Army Began Hotel Career." *Plain Dealer*, November 15, 1968.

Barrow, Bill. E-mail correspondence with author, August 17, 2020.

Bell, Erin, and James Calder. "Steve Dimotsis Interview." *Cleveland Voices*, June 9, 2008. https://clevelandvoices.org/items/show/2815.

Bellamy, Peter. "A Popular Restaurant Spot." *Plain Dealer*, Friday, August 20, 1976.

———. "Views of the Mixologists." *Plain Dealer*, September 24, 1976.

Beudert, Jason. "John Q's Steakhouse Closing." Cleveland Scene, May 23, 2013. https://www.clevescene.com/scene-and-heard/archives/2013/05/23/john-qs-steakhouse-closing.

Billboard Magazine (May 20, 1950): 4. Via GoogleBooks. https://books.google.com/books?id=VA4EAAAAMBAJ&printsec=frontcover#v=onepage&q=allerton&f=false.

Borsick, Helen. "Do You Remember?" *Plain Dealer*, June 13, 1971.

Brigotti, Rich. Phone interview with author, May 19, 1994.

Brown, Tony. "The Allen Theatre: A Timeline." *Plain Dealer*, June 6, 2010. https://www.cleveland.com/onstage/2010/06/the_allen_theatre_a_ timeline.html.

Bullard, Stan. "NY Spaghetti House in Downtown Cleveland Changes Hands." *Crain's Cleveland Business*, July 13, 2014.

Burdick, Ronald L., and Margaret L. Baughman. *Historic Photos of Cleveland*. Nashville, TN: Turner Publishing Company, 2007.

Carr, Kathy. "Most Memorable Restaurants of the Last 30 Years." *Crain's Cleveland Business*, May 25, 2010. https://www.crainscleveland.com/arti cle/20100525/30THANNIVERSARY/100219804/most-memorable-restaurants-of-the-last-30-years.

Charlie Christopherson website. "Biography." https://www. charliechristopherson.com/biography.

Chernin, Donna. "Find Key West on Huron Rd." *Plain Dealer*, Friday, January 23, 1987, 32.

Cicora, Elaine T. "Me and Chef Boyardee: How Cleveland's First Celebrity Chef Made Me the Woman I Am Today." Edible Cleveland. http:// ediblecleveland.com/stories/summer-2017/me-and-chef-boyardee.

Cleveland Area History. "Cleveland Nightlife in the 1930s?" October 20, 2011. http://www.clevelandareahistory.com/2011/10/cleveland-nightlife-in-1930s.html.

The Cleveland Blues Society—The Crossroads of Rust Belt Blues. "CBS Hall of Fame Biographies." http://www.clevelandblues.org/cbs-hall-of-fame/hall-of-fame-biographies.

Cleveland Gateway District. "Lower Prospect/Huron." http://www. clevelandgatewaydistrict.com/history/buildings-landmarks/lower-prospecthuron.

Cleveland Historical. "Bill Roberts Mural." https://clevelandhistorical.org/ index.php/files/show/7000.

———. "The Forum." Via Facebook, March 10, 2014. https://www. facebook.com/clevelandhistorical.

———. "May Company." https://clevelandhistorical.org/items/show/241.

Cleveland Magazine. "The Tong Wars" (February 23, 2008). https:// clevelandmagazine.com/in-the-cle/the-read/articles/the-tong-wars.

Cleveland Memory Project—Cleveland State University. "The Great Lakes Exposition." http://www.clevelandmemory.org/glihc/glexpo.

———. "Leedy Post Card." Postcards of Cleveland. Michael Schwartz Library, Special Collections. http://www.clevelandmemory.org.

Cleveland Plain Dealer. Advertisement, April 5, 1970.

———. Advertisement, July 19, 1961.

———. Advertisement, June 9, 1947.

———. Advertisement, June 30, 1885, 5.

———. Advertisement, March 24, 1940.

———. Advertisements, Thursday, April 14, 1938; Wednesday, April 10, 1940; February 17, 1943; Saturday, March 10, 1956; Wednesday, May 30, 1956; May 28, 1966; Thursday, June 22, 1967.

———. Allendorf Advertisements, February 21, 1904; June 1, 1919; March 10, 1924; January 21, 1934; July 4, 1936.

———. "Anniversary Day." June 23, 1888, 8.

———. "Announcing the Re-Creation of the Golden Pheasant." Advertisement, October 4, 1922.

———. "Another Attraction." October 30, 1887, 8.

———. "At Keith's Palace—The Week of November 9th—Austin Wylie and His Vocalian Recording Orchestra." Ad, November 5, 1924.

———. "Auctioning a Drink of History." May, 2, 1990, 21.

———. "The Boehmke Company Name Changed to that of the Real Owners." July 1, 1918.

———. "Café Opens in New Home." November 5, 1939.

———. "Chardon Sugar Festival—Suicide Johnny Meets Opponent— Aimee Bound for Holy Land." March 29, 1930.

———. "Cheeseburgers at W.T. Grant: Cleveland Remembers." May 12, 2011. https://www.cleveland.com/remembers/2011/05/cheeseburgers_at_wt_grant_clev.html.

———. Clark's ad, December 6, 1938, 6.

———. "Cleveland Mirrors Progress in New Rail Project." June 29, 1930.

———. "Closes Golden Pheasant Sale." August 15, 1926.

———. "Concert Singing Yields to 'Tea for Two' Tune." October 9, 1964, 98.

———. "Cosy [*sic*] and Secluded." May 15, 1887, 5.

———. "Daffy Entertainment from Paramount Gives Comedian Ben Blue His Big Chance." Friday, December 25, 1936, 22.

———. "Diners Raise Hollenden Roof." July 11, 1964, 2.

———. "Downbeat Club Padlock Sought." August 10, 1961, 45.

———. "Elegant Hog Saloon Ad." October 15, 1978.

———. "An Elegant Restaurant." February 12, 1888, 8.

———. "Enlarging the Philadelphia." September 25, 1887, 8.

———. "Erin Go Brrrrr! Bar Owner Misses Parade but Brings Permit." March 18, 1994.

———. The Finley System ad, April 4, 1908.

———. Fischer-Rohr Company ad, December 22 1918.

———. "Fischer-Rohr to Move to Chester." Cleveland. September 1, 1938.

———. "Fond Farewell." Cleveland, Ohio. April 5, 1990.

———. "George Jacobs, Restaurant Owner." Friday, August 4, 1978.

———. "German Tavern for Restaurant." October 27, 1938.

———. "Get Culinary Tips from Brother." August 24, 1937.

———. "Grand Opening." May 4, 1889.

———. "Hail Frontier! Deer, Bear on Menu; Now Bison Hangs on E. 9." December 20, 1936.

———. "He Opens New Café." May 3, 1936.

———. "Her Love Letters Aid Mrs. Finley to Win Divorce." Saturday, March 25, 1916, 1.

———. "Hundreds of Old Buildings Razed for Terminal." June 29, 1930.

———. "Into New Quarters." April 22, 1888.

———. "Isham Jones' Band Returning to Golden Pheasant April 4." March 29, 1931.

———. "Its Legs Are All Out of Proportion and It Walks in Kangaroo Fashion." January 19, 1903.

———. "Jacobs Takes Control of the Blue Boar Cafeteria." September 1, 1955.

———. "Lenihan Building Spot." N.d.

———. "Liquor Control Proposals Evoke Mixed Sentiment; Opposition Fears Rackets." November 18, 1933.

———. March 10, 1929, 6.

———. May Company ad, April 16, 1959, 3.

———. "A Metropolitan Institution." February 19, 1888, 8.

———. "New Hollenden to Make Bow Feb. 15." January 30, 1965, 40.

———. "Newman-Stern Moving; History Traced in PD." Thursday, November 9, 1967, 31.

———. "New York Muskie." August 29, 1937.

———. "9th St. Changes Have Made It Almost Perfect." July 05, 2011, http://blog.cleveland.com/pdextra/2011/07/9th_st_changes_have_made_it_al.html.

———. Obituary, John Henry Allendorf. July 27, 1948.

———. "Opening Monday the Spanish Room Restaurant-Tea Room." Ad, n.d.

————. "Parthenon Ad." July 4, 1980, 123.

————. "Parthenon Restaurant May Move." October 30, 1974, 68.

————. "Pheasant's 12th Anniversary." March 8, 1931.

————. "Pick Carter Spans Half Century." April 14, 1971, 10-E.

————. "Pirchner Is Night Manager." March 20, 1965, 13.

————. "Presidents et al Stayed at Pick Carter." April 15, 1971.

————. Purple Tree Lounge ad, April 24, 1970; June 26, 1970; August 27, 1972.

————. "R.G. Finley Dies; Ex-Restaurateur." January 3, 1937.

————. "Ray Boyle Back in Play House's 'Broken Quiet.'" November 12, 1950.

————. "Restaurant-Club Set Downtown." January 6, 1973, 5A.

————. "Rusty Scupper Restaurant Quietly Closes." April 3, 1984.

————. "Seasons Inaugurated at a Popular Place of Entertainment." September 18, 1887, 8.

————. "7 Die in Fire at Pick Carter." April 14, 1971.

————. "Shopping Comments by Kathryn." July 17, 1928; May 29, 1928; and February 4, 1929.

————. "Stouffer Corp. to Buy Rusty Scupper Chain." October 17, 1975, 6C.

————. "Sweet Water Waiters Sing at Supper." Friday, July 13, 1984.

————. "When Cleveland Had 2,475 Cafes!" March 24, 1933.

————. "Wild Rush to Escape Bullets Shooting Affray in Down Town Restaurant Caused Intense Excitement." September 10, 1904, 1.

————. "Woman's Touch Wins Friends." October 9, 1964.

Cleveland Town Topics. July 7, 1888, 4.

Coates, William R. "History of the Village of Cleveland, OH." In *A History of Cuyahoga County and the City of Cleveland*. Chicago and New York: American Historical Society, 1924.

Colebrook, Paul F., Jr. "The Hollenden House Revives Memories." *Plain Dealer*, March 21, 1965.

Collins, Holly. "French Connection Still a Classic." *Plain Dealer*, November 3, 1989.

Columbi, Chris, Jr. "Razzmatazz." *Plain Dealer*, May 9, 1980.

Company Histories. "Stouffer Corp." http://www.company-histories.com/Stouffer-Corp-Company-History.html.

Condon, George. *Prodigy of the Western Reserve*. Tulsa, OK: Continental Heritage Press Inc., 1979.

————. "Relish the Present and Feast on the Past." *Plain Dealer*, November 4, 1979.

Condon, George E. *Cleveland: The Best Kept Secret.* New York: Doubleday, 1967.

Crea, Joe. "Bricco-Cleveland Bows Out at Hanna Stage Is Set for a Hodge's Sibling to Debut in Playhouse Square." *Plain Dealer,* January 10, 2013.

———. "Chefs Go Wild With Girl Scout Cookies." *Plain Dealer,* October 12, 2011.

———. "Cleveland's Fat Fish Blue Restaurant to Close for Good Sunday." *Plain Dealer,* December 3, 2011. https://www.cleveland.com/dining/index.ssf/2011/12/clevelands_fat_fish_blue_resta.html.

———. "John Q's Steakhouse, a Downtown Cleveland Landmark, Will Close June 15: Restaurant Row." *Plain Dealer,* May 23, 2013. http://www.cleveland.com/dining/index.ssf/2013/05/john_qs_a_downtown_cleveland_l.html#incart_m-rpt-2.

Crump, Sarah. "Shaker Businesswoman, Volunteer Gets Kick Out of Unique Form of Dance." *Plain Dealer,* November 7, 2010.

D.L.M. "Lunch in the English Oak Room." *Along the Right of Way…The Ramblings of a Lifelong Model Railroader,* October 10, 2017.

Daily Tar Heel. "Kyser to Broadcast Over Station WTAM." March 31, 1931.

Dawson, Michelle. "The Stouffer Story." Unknown Stouffer publication.

DeAloia, Michael. E-mail correspondence with author, August 16, 2020.

———. *Lost Grand Hotels Of Cleveland.* Charleston, SC: The History Press, 2014.

———. "The May Company." Cool History. https://coolhistoryofcleveland.wordpress.com/2010/11/09/the-may-company.

DeLater, Laurie. "Sweetwater Café to Be Demolished." *Plain Dealer,* September 11, 1988.

DeMarco, Laura. *Lost Cleveland.* London: Pavilion Books, 2017.

———. "Vintage Cleveland Hotels: The Most Beautiful Spaces, Coolest Clubs, Most Colorful Stories." *Plain Dealer,* March 12, 2015. http://www.cleveland.com/entertainment/index.ssf/2015/03/clevelan.html.

Department Store Museum. "The Halle Bros. Company." http://www.thedepartmentstoremuseum.org/search?q=halle%27s.

DeVito, Chris, David Wild, Yasuhiro Fujioka and Wolf Schmaler. *The John Coltrane Reference.* Edited by Lewis Porter. New York: Routledge Taylor & Francis Group, 2013.

Dir, Dan, and Steve Dimotsis. Interview with the author, April 13, 2018.

Doty, Robert William, and Elizabeth Natalie Doty. *Man and Woman, War and Peace, 1942–1951: A Dual Autobiography, Verbatim from Their Letters and Diary.* New York: Vantage Press, 2004.

Du Jour, Jacques. "Don't Worry, Sans Souci Still in Top Form." *Morning Journal,* November 19, 1983.

Dutka, Alan F. *Cleveland's Short Vincent, the Theatrical Grill and Its Notorious Neighbors.* Cleveland, OH: Cleveland Landmarks Press, 2012.

———. *East Fourth Street.* Cleveland, OH: Cleveland Landmarks Press, 2011.

———. E-mail correspondence with the author, July 27, 2020.

———. *Historic Movie Theatres of Downtown Cleveland.* Charleston, SC: The History Press, 2016.

Escargot, Fourchette. "Nectar Sub Rosa." *Plain Dealer,* December 30, 1966.

Escargot, Yvonne. "Elegant English Oak Room Charms Our Gourmet Team." *Plain Dealer,* March 29, 1968.

Evans, Judith. "Gone but Not Forgotten: The Forum's Food Remains a Happy Memory for Many St. Louisans." *St. Louis Dispatch,* March 18, 1996.

Evett, Marianne. "Otto Moser's Tavern to the Stars." *Plain Dealer,* October 6, 1991.

Faith, Hope, and Remembrance: The Official Blog of the Catholic Cemeteries Association, Diocese of Cleveland. "Hector Boiardi: The Canned Pasta Creator." https://clevelandcatholiccemeteries.wordpress.com/2017/07/21/hector-boiardi-the-canned-pasta-creator.

French, Janet Beighle. "The Parthenon Is Spinning Gyros in Playhouse Square." *Plain Dealer,* March 22, 1974, 80–81.

———. "Rusty Scupper: Handy to Theatre and Parking." *Plain Dealer,* January 5, 1979.

Fried, Stephen. *Appetite for America: Fred Harvey and the Business of Civilizing the Wild West—One Meal at a Time.* New York: Bantam Books, 2011.

Gavin, Michael T. "The Great Lakes Exposition of 1936." *The Gamut,* no. 21 (Summer 1987). Cleveland State University.

Gerdel, Thomas W. "Euclid Burgerland." *Plain Dealer,* February 18, 1979.

Ghosts of Retailers Past. "Blue Boar Cafeteria." https://ghosts-of-retailers-past.fandom.com/wiki/Blue_Boar_Cafeteria.

Girl Scouts of North East Ohio. "Dessert First." https://www.gsneo.org/en/donate/signature-events/dessert-first-gala.html.

Glaser, Chris. "Gloria Lenihan." *Purple Armadillos,* June 25, 2010. http://purplearmadillos.blogspot.com/2010/06/chapter-5.html.

Gleisser, Marcus. "Downtown Shows Growth and New Life." *Plain Dealer,* July 7, 1974.

Great Lakes Theatre program. "Misery." February 16–March 11, 2018, 27.

H.J.B. "Forest City's Newest Hotel: Cleveland's Hotel Winton Is Opened—Another Palatial Hostelry Added to America's Finest." *Hotel World* 86, no. 1 (January 5, 1918): 29.

Hagenbaugh, Rachel. "Sex, Booze and Short Vincent Avenue." *Cleveland Magazine Blogspot*, August 3, 2011. http://clevelandmagazine.blogspot.com/2012/08/sex-booze-and-short-vincent-avenue.html.

Hamilton, Andrew. "Bobby Wade, Artist Biography." All Music. https://www.allmusic.com/artist/bobby-wade-mn0001917433/biography.

Hansen, David. "Chef Boyardee." *Cleveland Centennial Blog*, May 2011. http://clevelandcentennial.blogspot.com/2011/05/chef-boyardee.html.

Hardin, Angela Y. "Fat Fish Blue Restaurant to Resurface: Former May Co. Parking Garage to House Eatery." *Crain's Cleveland Business*, October 27, 1997.

Hatcher, Harlan. *The Western Reserve*. Cleveland, OH: World Publishing Company, 1949 and 1966.

Heaton, Michael. *Truth and Justice for Fun and Profit*. Cleveland, OH: Gray & Company, 2007.

Herrick, Clay, Jr. *Cleveland Landmarks*. Cleveland, OH: Cleveland Landmarks Commission, 1986.

Hickey, William. "Marie Schreiber." *Plain Dealer*, December 18, 1970.

Hickok, Ralph J. "On the Road Again and Again…." *Sports Illustrated*, September 9, 1987. https://www.si.com/vault/1987/09/09/116134/on-the-road-again-and-again----in-117-days-during-1926-27-duluth-played-29-games----27-away.

Higgins, Bette Lou. "Whose Idea Was That?" Program script. Elyria, OH: Eden Valley Enterprises, 2009.

Hirschfeld, Mary. "The Roof Is the Limit at New Hollenden's Party." *Plain Dealer*, July 7, 1964, 15.

———. "Serving Up a Sax Solo for Dessert." *Plain Dealer*, Friday, January 23, 1987.

Historical Collections of the Great Lakes. "The *Kearsarge*." https://greatlakes.bgsu.edu/item/436137.

Hotel World 88, no. 15. "Announce Opening of Mills Restaurant" (April 12, 1919): 10.

Hotel World 88, no. 6. "Hotel Winton Shows New Film Offerings" (February 8, 1919): 8.

House-Soremekun, Bessie. *Confronting the Odds: African American Entrepreneurship in Cleveland, Ohio*. Kent, OH: Kent State University Press, 2002.

Hub Biz. "John Q's Steakhouse." https://john-q-s-steakhouse.hub.biz.

Husband, Stuart. "The Duke of Beverly Hills: Adolphe Menjou." *The Rake: The Modern Voice of Classic Elegance*, December 2016. https://therake.com/stories/icons/the-duke-of-beverly-hills-adolphe-menjou.

Jarboe, Michelle. "New York Spaghetti House Could Be Razed, as Geis Plots Downtown Cleveland Project." *Plain Dealer*, July 23, 2015. https://www.cleveland.com/business/index.ssf/2015/07/new_york_spaghetti_house_could.html.

Jeeves & Fork. "Mamma and Otto." March 19, 2017. https://www.jeevesandfork.com/mamma-and-otto.

Jerry's Brokendown Palaces. "Allen Theatre, 1501 Euclid Ave, Cleveland, OH." September 9, 2011. http://jerrygariasbrokendownpalaces.blogspot.com/2011/09/allen-theater-1501-euclid-ave-cleveland.html.

Jindra, Christine J. "Playhouse Square Pulse Beats Faster." *Plain Dealer*, June 10, 1977, 1.

Karberg, Richard E., and James A. Toman. *Euclid Ave: Cleveland's Sophisticated Lady, 1920–1970*. Cleveland, OH: Cleveland Landmarks Press, 2002.

Karberg, Richard E., Judith Karberg and Jane Hazen. *The Silver Grille: Memories*. Cleveland, OH: Cleveland Landmarks Press, 2000.

Kelly, S.J. "Old Restaurants in Cleveland." *Cleveland Plain Dealer*, September 16, 1937.

Klein, Richard, PhD. "'Let's Go Shopping at the Square': Cleveland's Leading Downtown Department Stores—A Business Legacy." Michael Schwartz Library, Cleveland State University, 2014.

Klien, Christopher. "The Surprising History of the Real Chef Boy-Ar-Dee." History, 2015. http://www.history.com/news/hungry-history/the-surprising-history-of-the-real-chef-boy-ar-dee.

Krantz, John. "Uniquely Greek." *Plain Dealer*, December 7, 1988, 181.

L.N.B. "Corned Beef." *The Breeder's Gazette: A Weekly Journal for the American Stock Farm* 55, no. 2 (January 13, 1909): 1,416, 79.

The Ladies of Saint Anselm's Church. *San Anselmo Cook-Book*. Bedford, MA: Applewood Books, 1908.

Lee, Laura. "He's the Chef." *The Scene*, September 23, 1999. https://www.clevescene.com/cleveland/hes-the-chef/Content?oid=1472837.

Lemoore, Hanford. "Tiki Central." Tiki Room. http://www.tikiroom.com/tikicentral/bb/viewtopic.php?topic=32516&forum=2.

Lesie, Michele. "From Swamp to Industrial Center." *Plain Dealer Magazine* (January 13, 1991).

Livingston, Tom. "Video Vault: Remembering Cleveland's Captain Frank's Restaurant." Newsnet5, November 5, 2012. Newsnet5.com.

Llanas, Sheila Griffin. *Ettore Boiardi: Chef Boyardee Manufacturer*. Minneapolis, MN: ABDO Publishing Company, 2015.

Long, John S. "The Caxton Cafe Soap Opera." *Plain Dealer*, November 6, 1996, 3F.

———. "Despite Recent Closings, Downtown Scene Is Lively." *Plain Dealer*, November 27, 1996, 3E.

Loveland, Roelif. "Buffalo Rustling Foiled Downtown." *Plain Dealer*, December 18, 1938.

———. "On Old New Year Another Little Drink Did No Harm." *Cleveland Plain Dealer*, Wednesday, December 31, 1930.

Magicpedia. "Luxor Gali-Gali." https://geniimagazine.com/wiki/index.php?title=Luxor_Gali-Gali.

Maharidge, Dale. "Happy Hours." *Plain Dealer*, May 30, 1980.

Marsh, Ward, and Ed. Kuekes. "Close-Ups." *Plain Dealer*, October 17, 1948.

Mayfair Casino postcard. Cleveland State University Cleveland Memory Project. http://images.ulib.csuohio.edu/cdm/singleitem/collection/postcards/id/32/rec/1.

McDermott, William F. "Ring Theater Will Put on Moss Hart's Satiric Comedy, 'Light Up the Sky.'" *Plain Dealer*, August 27, 1950.

McFarland, Rebecca. "Eliot Ness and His Role in Cleveland History." Cleveland Police Museum, January 2012. http://www.clevelandpolicemuseum.org/collections/eliot-ness.

———. "Leonard Schlather, 1835–1918." Unpublished manuscript, Rocky River Library, June 1995.

Mellow, Jan. "Bulldozers Halt, Save an Old Man's Garden." *Plain Dealer*, Saturday, May 14, 1960.

———. "They're Slicin' Bison at New Hotel Carter Saloon." *Cleveland Plain Dealer*, September 29, 1956, 8.

Miller, Marylin. "Short Vincent." Cleveland Historical, September 22, 2010. https://clevelandhistorical.org/items/show/64.

Miller, William F. "Allen's 'Phantom' to Be Chef There." *Plain Dealer*, Friday, February 11, 1977.

———. "New Buildings Keep Changing Downtown Skyline." *Plain Dealer*, September 22, 1974.

———. "Playhouse Square Future Rosy." *Plain Dealer*, January 1, 1975.

Monnett, James G., Jr. "Euclid—E. 13th St. Gets Restaurant." *Plain Dealer*, November 22, 1935, 28:3.

Moore, Opha. "Biography of James O. Mills." *History of Franklin County, Ohio*. Topeka, KS: Historical Publishing Company, 1930. Via Online Biographies, http://www.onlinebiographies.info/oh/frank/mills-jo.htm.

Morgan, Jon. *Glory for Sale: Fans, Dollars, and the New NFL*. Baltimore, MD: Bancroft Press, 1997.

Mosbrook, Joe. *Cleveland Jazz History*. 2nd ed. Cleveland: Northeast Ohio Jazz Society, 2003.

———. "Cleveland: Part 38." *Jazzed in Cleveland*, WMV Web News, June 22, 1998. http://www.cleveland.oh.us/wmv_news/jazz38.htm.

———. "Cleveland: Part 49—Some Historic Cleveland Jazz Clubs." *Jazzed in Cleveland*, WMV Web News, January 3, 2000. http://www.cleveland.oh.us/wmv_news/jazz49.htm.

———. "Cleveland: Part 102—The Cleveland Cotton Club." *Jazzed in Cleveland*, WMV Web News. http://www.cleveland.oh.us/wmv_news/jazz102.htm.

———. "Cleveland: Part 122—The Role Of Radio." *Jazzed in Cleveland*, WMV Web News, October 13, 2008. http://www.cleveland.oh.us/wmv_news/jazz122.htm.

———. "Cleveland: Part 134—The Jazz Corner of Cleveland." *Jazzed in Cleveland*, WMV Web News. http://www.cleveland.oh.us/wmv_news/jazz134.htm.

Moser, Emily. "A Visit to the Former Cleveland Union Terminal." I Ride the Harlem Line, July 19, 2013. http://www.iridetheharlemline.com/2013/07/19/a-visit-to-the-former-cleveland-union-terminal.

Mottor, Laura, and Kimberly Graves. E-mail correspondence with author, July 21, 2020.

Motz, Doug, and Christine Hayes. *Lost Restaurants of Columbus, Ohio*. Charleston, SC: The History Press, 2015.

Murphey, Fran. "Onion-Ring Lovers Can Thank Wertheim." *Akron Beacon Journal*, June 13, 1985.

Neale, Natalie. "The Schofield Building: Recovering the Original Façade." Cleveland Historical. https://clevelandhistorical.org/items/show/812.

Nestlé. "That's One Giant Leap for Stouffer's!" https://www.nestle.com/aboutus/history/nestle-company-history/stouffers.

Newark Advocate. "News Digest." Tuesday, November 21, 1882, 6.

Newbold, Allison V. "Hollenden Hotel." Cleveland Historical. https://clevelandhistorical.org/items/show/818.

New York City Landmarks Preservation Commission. *Designation List 402 LP–2296*. March 18, 2008.

New York Times. "Hector Boiardi Is Dead: Began Chef Boy-Ar-Dee." June 23, 1985. https://www.nytimes.com/1985/06/23/us/hector-boiardi-is-dead-began-chef-boy-ar-dee.html.

Nowak, Matt. "New York Spaghetti House, Cleveland Ohio." History Every Day, January 13, 2016. http://www.historyeveryday.org/new-york-spaghetti-house--ohio.html.

Nyerges, Scott. "Yesterday: W.T. Grant and Co." *Classic Five-and-Dime Stores* (blog). Cheapism, January 17, 2020. https://blog.cheapism.com/classic-five-and-dime-stores/#slide=6.

O'Connor, Clint. "'In' Joint Shifts." *Plain Dealer*, February 6, 1994.

Ohio Burlesque. "A Remarkable Memory." https://www.ohioburlesque.com/the-cleveland-roxy.html.

Orth, Samuel Peter. *A History of Cleveland, Ohio: Biographical.* Chicago: S.J. Clarke Publishing Company, 1910.

Ott, Thomas. "LeanDog, Arras Owners Buy Former Hornblower's Restaurant." *Plain Dealer*, July 22, 2011. http://blog.cleveland.com/metro/2011/07/leandog_software_firm_buys_for.html.

Owen, Lorri K., ed. *Ohio Historic Places Dictionary.* Vol. 2. Clair Shores, MI: Somerset Publishers Inc., 1999.

Pearsall, Shelley. "Brothers." *Classic Clevelanders.* Elyria, OH: Eden Valley Enterprises, n.d.

Petrovic, John. "Bringing the City into Perspective." *Plain Dealer*, July 10, 2010.

Phadie, Heesa. "History of Stouffer's Restaurants & Hotels." *Eating the Road*, November 12, 2009. https://eatingtheroad.wordpress.com/restaurant-list/history-of-stouffers-resturants-hotels.

Pinkerton, Richard L., PhD, and Charles T. Roehl. *The Historic Private Clubs and Restaurants of Cleveland, Ohio.* Cleveland, OH: Western Reserve Historical Society Library, n.d.

Plaster, Joey. "Behind the Masks: LGBT Lives at Oberlin College from the 1920s to the Early 1970s." Oberlin LGBT, 2006. http://www.oberlinlgbt.org/wp-content/uploads/2015/12/BehindtheMasks.pdf.

Pohlen, Jerome. *Oddball Ohio: A Guide to Some Really Strange Places.* Chicago: Chicago Review Press, 2004.

Pullen, Glen. "England's Ted Heath to Play Concert Here." *Plain Dealer*, January 13, 1957.

———. "Woody, D'Lacy Band Form Their Own Rules." *Plain Dealer*, September 20, 1959.

Pullen, Glenn C. "Done with Mirrors." *Plain Dealer*, Sunday, October 20, 1946.

————. "Footlights and Bright Lights." *Plain Dealer*, May 22, 1936.

————. "Mayfair Builds Sidewalk Café; Skits for Showboat." *Plain Dealer*, Sunday, July 4, 1937.

————. "Mayfair Opens Today; Vogue Room's Revue." *Cleveland Plain Dealer*, Friday, December 25, 1936.

————. "Summer Theaters Spring Up with Luring List of Shows." *Plain Dealer*, June 25, 1950.

————. "Sweeter Music in Cafés and Higher Standards in Acts Developed by 1938." *Plain Dealer*, January 1, 1939.

————. "Vaughn Monroe, Palace Star, Recalls Days When He Was in Austin Wylie's Band Here." *Plain Dealer*, March 5, 1946.

————. "Walberg's Ensemble Breaks a Fischer-Rohr Tradition; Lake Opens Sterling Room." *Plain Dealer*, November 27, 1938.

Reece, Cynthia. "Elegant Hog Features Satisfaction." *Plain Dealer*, June 30, 1978.

Relihan, Cecil. "Hard-to-Get Figures Are Reflection of Italian Family's Love of Beauty." *Plain Dealer*, June 2, 1964.

————. "Marie Schreiber Proud of Tavern." *Plain Dealer*, March 21, 1965.

Renaissance Cleveland Hotel. "Uniquely Renaissance." Hotel publication, date unknown.

Revolvy. "Parkview Apartments (Cleveland)." https://www.revolvy.com/main/index.php?s=Parkview%20Apartments%20(Cleveland).

Rice, Gary. "Lakewood's Theater Hero, Weldon Carpenter…What One Person Can Do." *Lakewood Observer* 10, no. 10 (May 13, 2014). http://lakewoodobserver.com/read/2014/05/13/lakewoods-theater-hero-weldon-carpenter-what-one-person-can-do.

Rich, Marci. "The Silver Grille's Maurice Salad." The Midlife Second Wife™, May 31, 2013. https://themidlifesecondwife.com/2013/05/31/the-silver-grilles-maurice-salad.

Robinson, Amelia. "Dayton's Little-Known Cheezy Past." Dayton, April 25, 2020. https://www.dayton.com/blog/seen-and-overheard/were-cheez-its-really-invented-dayton-yes-and-here-the-story/w4gZxZzIAczWdUSR2ow71I.

Robison, W. Scott, ed. *History of the City of Cleveland: Its Settlement, Rise and Progress*. Cleveland, OH: Robison & Crocket, 1887.

Rocco, Roberta. E-mail correspondence with author, June 29, 2020.

Roehl, Charles T. Letter to author, May 28, 2019.

Roehl, Tom. Interview with author, September 28, 2018.

Rose, William Ganson. *Cleveland: The Making of a City*. Cleveland, OH: World Publishing Company, 1950.

Roy, Chris. "The Last Moving Picture Company." Cleveland Historical. https://clevelandhistorical.org/items/show/891.

Ruhlman, Michael. *The Soul of a Chef: The Journey Toward Perfection*. New York: Penguin Books, 2001.

Russo, Gus. *Supermob: How Sidney Korshak and His Criminal Associates Became America's Hidden Power Brokers*. New York: Bloomsbury, 2006.

Sabath, Donald. "Downtown Is Verging on New Glory." *Plain Dealer*, January 14, 1974.

Salem News. "Freddie Is Robbed." April 24, 1940, 5.

Salisbury, Wilma. "Glory Days Not Over for Hickerson's Eatery." *Plain Dealer*, November 24, 1995.

———. "The Many Faces of a Downtown Restaurant." *Plain Dealer*, May 5, 1985.

———. "Parthenon Misses Downton." *Plain Dealer*, December 30, 1988, 85.

Scott, Jane. "Jazz Club to Open on Playhouse Square." *Plain Dealer*, August 11, 1991.

———. "She Keeps 88 Keys to Happiness." *Plain Dealer*, September 9, 1962, 128.

Segall, Grant. "Bob Wertheim, Owned Restaurants, Loved Jokes." *Plain Dealer*, April 14, 2009. https://www.cleveland.com/obituaries/index.ssf/2009/04/bob_wertheim.html.

Smith, Christian. "The Hanna Building." Cleveland Historical, December 7, 2017. https://clevelandhistorical.org/items/show/827.

Smith, Jordan. "Top of the Town—Cleveland, Ohio." Cardboard America, October 12, 2016. https://cardboardamerica.org/2016/10/12/stouffers.

Smith, Leonard W. "Finley's—Yes—Finley's." *Printers' Ink* 63, no. 3 (April 15, 1908): 32.

Snook, Debbi. "Bricco Will Get You to the Show on Time and Mostly Satisfied." *Plain Dealer*, July 4, 2008.

———. "The Gala Great Lakes Expo." *Cleveland Plain Dealer*, August 4, 1996.

———. "Pick 3." *Plain Dealer, Friday! Magazine* (July 25, 2008).

Stamper, John W. *Chicago's North Michigan Avenue: Planning and Development, 1900–1930*. Chicago: University of Chicago Press, 1991.

Strassmeyer, Mary. "Fond Farewell." *Plain Dealer*, July 22, 1988.

———. "The Line Forms on Euclid." *Plain Dealer*, Sunday, June 17, 1973, E1, E6.

———. "Mary, Mary." *Plain Dealer*, Friday, July 11, 1984.

———. "Mary, Mary." *Plain Dealer*, January 15, 1988.

———. "Mary, Mary." *Plain Dealer*, November 6, 1978.

———. "Mary, Mary." *Plain Dealer*, September 11, 1992.

———. "Mary, Mary." *Plain Dealer*, Tuesday, October 23, 1984.

———. "Psst!" *Plain Dealer*, May 20, 1984.

———. "Sweetwater Swan Song Moved Up." *Plain Dealer*, Wednesday, August 24, 1988.

Students in Conference—The Chinese Students Alliance, Mid-West Section, U.S.A. "Public Entertainment." Program book. Ohio State University, September 5–6, 1919.

Stutz, Marie. "New York Spaghetti House Reopened 2004!" Modern Cleveland. http://moderncleveland.com/restaurants/nysh.

Sullivan, Jack. "Fred Diebolt and Cleveland's Saloonkeeper Revolt." *Those Pre-Pro Whiskey Men!*, March 18, 2017. http://pre-prowhiskeymen.blogspot.com/2017/03/fred-diebolt-and-clevelands.html.

Sunday Plain Dealer. "New Inn Will Be a Downtown Spa." January 29, 1978.

Teaching Cleveland Digital. "Posthumous Inductees to Inside Business Cleveland Business Hall of Fame." http://teachingcleveland.org/cleveland-business-hall-of-fame-inside-business-good-list.

Thebeau, Mark, PhD, and Mark Souther, PhD, Executive Producers. "That Was My First Experience Over on Short Vincent" (speaker anonymous). Oral history audio by Cleveland State University Department of History for Public History and Digital Humanities. Cleveland Regional Oral History Collection, 2010.

Thompson, Ian. Interview with the author, August 30, 2019.

Till, Michael J. *Along Ohio's Historic Route 20*. Charleston, SC: Arcadia Publishing, 2013.

Tim. "A Fat Fish Blue Adventure." Big Beef and Beer, circa 2000. http://bigbeefandbeer.com/adventure.htm.

Trickey, Erick. "Renaissance Cleveland Hotel, 1918." *Cleveland Magazine* (November 18, 2011). https://clevelandmagazine.com/in-the-cle/articles/renaissance-cleveland-hotel-1918-.

Vacha, John. *The Best Barber in America*. Teaching Cleveland Digital. http://teachingcleveland.org/the-best-barber-in-america-by-john-vacha.

———. *Meet Me On Lake Erie, Dearie!* Kent, OH: Kent State University Press, 2011.

———. *The Music Went 'Round and Around: The Story of Musicarnival*. Kent, OH: Kent State University Press, 2004.

————. *Showtime in Cleveland: The Rise of a Regional Theater Center*. Kent, OH: Kent State University Press, 2001.

Van Tassel, David D., and John J. Grabowski, eds. *Encyclopedia of Cleveland History*. Bloomington: Indiana University Press, 1987 and 1996.

Variety. "Corio-'Personal' Hold 3d Wk. in Cleve Ring." August 2, 1950.

Vexler, Robert I., ed. *Cleveland: A Chronological and Documentary History, 1760–1976*. Dobbs Ferry, NY: Oceana Publications Inc., 1977.

Von Dobeneck, Alisa. "How to Make Presidential Hash." The Daily Beast, July 12, 2017. https://www.thedailybeast.com/how-to-make-presidential-hash.

Ward, Michael. "Now Boukair Takes Bite at New 'Apple.'" *Plain Dealer*, Action Tab, Friday, March 29, 1974.

West High Cleveland. "Boukair's." Updated August 3, 2014. https://sites.google.com/site/clevelandwesthigh1962/nostalgia/boukairs.

Whitaker, Jan. "The Brotherhood of the Beefsteak Dungeon." *Restaurant-ing through History* (blog), November 19, 2008. https://restaurant-ingthroughhistory.com.

————. "A Hair in the Soup." *Restaurant-ing through History*, November 19, 2016. https://restaurant-ingthroughhistory.com/2016/11/19/a-hair-in-the-soup.

Wiggins, Allen. "English Oak Room's Smitty Dies at 79." *Plain Dealer*, May 21, 1973.

Wikipedia. "Ettore Boiardi." https://en.wikipedia.org/wiki/Ettore_Boiardi.

————. "55 Public Square." https://en.wikipedia.org/wiki/55_Public_Square.

————. "George F. Hammond." https://en.wikipedia.org/wiki/George_F._Hammond.

————. "The Great Lakes Exposition." https://en.wikipedia.org/wiki/Great_Lakes_Exposition.

————. "Halle Building." https://en.wikipedia.org/wiki/Halle_Building.

————. "Hollenden Hotel." https://en.wikipedia.org/wiki/Hollenden_Hotel.

————. "Sterling-Lindner Co." https://en.wikipedia.org/wiki/Sterling-Lindner_Co.

————. "Winton Manor." https://en.wikipedia.org/wiki/Winton_Manor.

————. "W.T. Grant." https://en.wikipedia.org/wiki/W._T._Grant.

William T. Grant Foundation. http://wtgrantfoundation.org/history.

Willy, John. "Cleveland's New $4,000,000 Hotel Cleveland." *Hotel Monthly* 27, no. 311 (February, 1919): 145.

———. "Unique Restaurant in Cleveland, Ohio." *Hotel Monthly* 27, no. 314 (May 1919): 60.

Wood, G. Zay, Editor in Chief, and K.C. Sun, General Manager. *The Chinese Student's Monthly* 16 (November, 1920–June 1921).

Wood, James M. *Halle's Memories of a Family Department Store, 1891–1982.* Cleveland, OH: Geranium Press, 1987.

Index

A

A. Jacob's Grill Room 145
Allendorf's Chop House 33
Allerton Hotel 36
Alpine Village 12, 40, 42, 73, 89
Anders Cafeteria 124
Apres Vous 124

B

Bismark Café and Grotto 15
Black Angus 30, 153, 160, 164
Blue Boar 60, 61, 62
Boiardi, Ettore (Hector) 10, 26, 95, 96, 97, 181
Boukair's See Sweets Restaurant 30, 43, 46
Bronze Room 169, 170, 171

C

Cadillac Lounge 12, 16
Café on the Square 170
Café Windsor 121
Captain Frank's Seafood House 30, 48, 50, 141
Casino Restaurant 51
Caxton Café 54, 55, 56
Chef Hector's 97
Childs Restaurant 58, 78
Clark's Coffee Shop 58
Clark's Colonial 57
Clark's Dairy Lunch 57
Clark's Paul Revere House 23, 58
Clark's Restaurants 57, 59, 74, 78
Cloverleaf Restaurants 60
Club Carnival 145, 146
Colonial Tea Room 138
Columbia Restaurant 19
Coney Island, the 144, 156
Continental Room 77

Cotton Club 121, 122
Craddock, Harry 88

D

Daisy Café 121
Danny's Bar 146
De Paree Bar 147
Diebolt, Fred 27, 28, 29

E

Ed Rafferty's Museum 24
Elbow Room 145
Elegant Hog Saloon 19
English Oak Room 175, 176, 179
Euclid Avenue Opera House 110,
    111, 113, 121, 126
Exposition Cafeteria 74

F

Fat Fish Blue 20
Feichtmeier Restaurant 121
Ferris Steakhouse 124
Finley's 63, 64, 65, 66, 67
Fireside Inn 145
Fischer-Rohr ("Rohr's") 35, 68, 69,
    150
Flannery's Pub 126
Forum, the 20, 21, 30
Freddie's Café/Freddie's Paradise
    Café 145, 151
Freddie's Paradise Café 145
French Connection 162, 163, 170,
    171

French Quarter 145
Frolics, the 145, 146
Frosty Bar 135

G

Gaslight Room 159, 160
George Rassie Restaurant 124
George's Bar 145
Geranium Room 138
Getty's at the Hanna 80
Gigi's 124
Gilsey Hotel 147
Golden Pheasant 70, 71, 72
Grant's 127, 128
Great Lakes Exposition 27, 73, 76,
    87
Grecian Gardens 123
Grogshop, the 146

H

Halle Bros. 132, 135, 136, 137,
    138, 139, 141
Hanna, Allie 54
Hanna Building 30, 57, 77, 81, 120
Hanna, Joe 54
Hanna, Marcus (Mark) 84, 86
Hanna Pub 78, 79
Harvey Company 175
Harvey Girls 175, 178, 179
Herman Pirchner's Alpine Village
    Show Boat 73
Hickerson's 80
Hickory Grill 145
Higbee's 131, 133, 134, 135, 139,
    140, 141, 175, 177

Hollenden House/Hotel 18, 25, 52, 83, 84, 86, 87, 88, 89, 90, 101, 129, 143, 151, 153
Hornblower's Barge & Grille 91, 93
Hotel Cleveland 168, 169, 170, 171, 175
Hustler Club 146

I

Il Giardino d'Italia 95, 96
Italian Renaissance Men's Grille 138

J

John Q's Public Bar & Grille 159, 160, 163

K

Kon-Tiki 171, 172, 177, 178
Kornman's 68, 144, 147, 150, 151, 153
Kornman's Back Room 144
Kornman, William 147

L

Last Moving Picture Company 21, 22
Le Bistro 135

M

Mandarin Tea Room 138
May Company 20, 80, 128, 129, 130, 132
Mayfair Casino 98, 100
Mayfair Room/Mayfair Restaurant 129, 130, 132
McCrory's 127
McGlade's 4th Street Restaurant 121
Mickey's Lounge Bar 146, 147
Mickey's Show Bar 144, 146
Mills Restaurant 101, 102
Minotaur Room 132, 138, 141
Monaco, the 76, 77
Monkey House 24
Moser, Otto 12, 26, 110, 111, 113, 114, 116, 121
Mowry's 167
Myers, George 83, 84, 86

N

New Dairy Lunch 57
New York Spaghetti House 12, 103, 104, 105, 163

O

Old Allen Theatre Restaurant 108
Opera House Café 121
Otto Moser's 16, 110, 111, 114, 116, 121

P

Parisian Bar 147
Parthenon, the 43, 44
Persian Lounge 123
Pewter Mug 12, 78, 118, 120
Philadelphia Dairy and Café 22, 23
Pickwick 16, 60, 62, 147
Pierre's Italian Restaurant 43, 44, 97
Pony's Café 147
Pronto Room 135

R

Rafferty, Ed 24
Rathskeller, the 27, 30, 121, 126
Renaissance Cleveland 11, 168, 171
Rose Room 169
Roundtable 51, 53
Roxy Bar & Grille 157, 162
Roxy's Café 124
Roxy, the 147, 156, 157
Rusty Scupper 30, 108, 160, 162,
    164, 166

S

Savoy Cocktail Book 88
730 Lounge 147
Sheraton Cleveland 168, 170, 178
Short Vincent 62, 83, 88, 143, 144,
    145, 146, 147, 150, 151, 152,
    153, 156, 157, 162
Silver Grille 131, 132, 133, 134,
    135, 140, 141, 142
Spanish Room Restaurant and Tea
    Room 129

Star Bar and Grill 124
Sterling-Lindner-Davis 130, 131
Stouffer, Abraham 158
Stouffer, Gordon 158
Stouffer, Mahala 158
Stouffer Renaissance Cleveland
    168, 171
Stouffer's Inn on the Square 168,
    170
Stouffer's Lunch 162
Stouffer's Restaurants 158
Stouffer's Tower City Plaza 168
Stouffer, Vernon 158
Streets of the World 73, 74
Sweetwater Café 162, 164, 165

T

Tavern Chop House 12, 25, 89
Taystee-Bar-B-Q 145
Terminal Tower 131, 132, 140,
    141, 142, 162, 167, 173, 175,
    177, 178
Theatrical Grill/The Theatrical
    88, 144, 145, 151, 152, 153,
    157
Top of the Town 160, 162, 163
Town Pump Bar 147

W

Weber's 15, 27, 51, 53
Weinberger, Isadore 147
Winton-Carter Hotel 180
Wishbone Restaurant 145
Woolworth's 127, 139, 140, 141

About the Author

B ette Lou Higgins has an MEd from Cleveland State University and a BA from Baldwin-Wallace College. She is the artistic director and a founder of Eden Valley Enterprises (EVE), where she has been involved in researching, writing, producing and performing more than forty original productions. Specializing in historical programs, EVE's repertoire covers topics such as the Great Depression, World War II, the Great Lakes and profiles of historic figures often neglected by mainstream media. The company has also done a number of women's history presentations. Find out more at www.edenvalleyenterprises.org.

Photo by Lindsay Yost Bott.